Also by Glenn Wilson

LOVE AND ATTRACTION: AN INTERNATIONAL CONFERENCE
  (with M. Cook)

THE MYSTERY OF LOVE: THE HOWS AND WHYS OF SEXUAL
  ATTRACTION
  (with David Nias)

PSYCHOLOGY OF SEX
  (with H. J. Eysenck)

SECRETS OF SEXUAL FANTASY

Sexual Variations

Fetishism, Sadomasochism and Transvestism

Chris Gosselin, Ph.D.
& Glenn Wilson, Ph.D.

SIMON AND SCHUSTER

NEW YORK

Published by Simon and Schuster
A Division of Gulf & Western Corporation
Simon & Schuster Building
Rockefeller Center
1230 Avenue of the Americas
New York, New York 10020

SIMON AND SCHUSTER and colophon are trademarks of
Simon & Schuster
Manufactured in the United States of America

Originally published in Great Britain in 1980 by Faber and Faber Ltd.

1   2   3   4   5   6   7   8   9   10

Library of Congress Cataloging in Publication Data
Gosselin, Chris.
Sexual variations.

Bibliography: p.
Includes index.
1. Fetishism. 2. Sadism. 3. Masochism.
4. Transvestism. I. Wilson, Glenn Daniel,
joint author. II. Title.
HQ79.G67   306.7   80-19084
ISBN 0-671-24624-0

Contents

Introduction

Within the last few years, the publication of "sexy" books and magazines has become a multi-million dollar industry. Some of these publications are straightforward girlie magazines, these alone selling hundreds of millions of copies per year; some walk delicately—or indelicately—along the wavering tightrope between acceptability and potential prosecution; others are unashamedly pornographic. All these books and magazines, however, have in common the fact that they are consumer-oriented, designed to give pleasure to those who buy and read them.

For a different audience, psychiatrists, psychologists and others have been publishing their experiences with "patients" for whom the sexuality that fills the pages of sexy magazines is more a problem than a pleasure. These professionals have published articles and case-histories, generally interpreting the latter according to their own beliefs. In doing so, they have tended to foster an assumption that people whose sexual patterns do not conform to a rather ill-defined idea of the "conventional" are automatically people with problems.

Of course, as society stands, this view is partly correct. One

cannot possess a sexual desire for children without having a
problem; one cannot possess, as a prelude to sexual release, a
desire to cause unacceptable pain or kill another being, without having a problem. Nevertheless, the increasing openness
with which ordinary men and women nowadays admit that
their sexual intimacies do not always move straight from first
kiss to intercourse, alerts us to the fact that not every variation
produces in its practitioner a specter of guilt or anxiety, or is
regarded by him as a "problem." Not every husband—or wife
—who in fact or fantasy affectionately smacks his or her partner's behind during the prelude to lovemaking is labeled a
sadist, and not every woman who undresses slowly in front of
her lover thinks of him as a Peeping Tom, or of herself as an
exhibitionist. Not every man who adds an element of forceful-
ness to intercourse while his partner whispers, "Get off, you
—!" is condemned by either party as a rapist, nor does every
man who with mounting arousal watches a pair of long,
leather, high-heeled boots clicking up the escalator in front of
him regard himself as a pathological fetishist.

Nevertheless, the awareness of the probability that *most*
people have a liking for something a little different sexually
has been almost entirely instinctive. In spite of people's
greater willingness to speak about themselves, medical science has not really seized the opportunity to study the general
world of sexual variations, because, in fairness, it has been
much too busy treating those for whom sex variations consti-
tute a problem. Problems create fear and silence and the person who believes that others might disapprove of his sexual
pattern fears the social contact which might confirm that dis-
approval. He even fears that those who might in fact be able
to relieve his anxiety might not understand, might reject. As a
result, only the most disturbed, the most deeply hurt and the
most desperate are driven to brave the portals of official help-
centers to obtain such relief as might be available. Medical
people report only on those whom they see; the spectrum of
sexual variation, and those who practice it, is thus seen by the
medical researcher and practitioner more or less entirely from
its most extreme end.

Freud, of course, had a lot to say about general sexual behavior and wrote about the sadomasochism, fetishism and exploration of sex roles that he believed to be part of everyone's makeup. To his credit, he was one of the few people writing about sex in his day who saw in the everyday behavior of ordinary people the possible roots of these so-called aberrant behaviors, postulating the idea of a spectrum of sexual activity from the conventional to the highly unusual. Some psychologists think he overdid it, and in any case many people confused the issue by taking Freud's ideas and theories for unarguable fact—which they weren't. The contributions that he and others made at the time were observations of a number of cases, pulled together into a systematic but *untested* whole. The theories which arose largely as a result of armchair thinking, were intended as plausible explanations of what had been observed. They were seldom tested by setting up experimental situations to find out when they were supported and when not.

As a result, it was fatally easy for theorists like Freud to illustrate their theories, however right they might be, only with material that supported their views, or to attribute contrary evidence to some other cause. In later years, during the "swinging sixties," there grew up a strange state of affairs wherein science had many theories about sexual variations, based largely on nonrepresentative samples of the populace, while most of society was beginning to realize that variations were a lot more commonplace than had previously been believed, and were practiced by very ordinary people. Still, there were few theories about how, and why, and when, and to whom these variations came about.

However, about this time, psychologists (who study everyone they can lay their hands on, as opposed to psychiatrists, who are medical men more concerned with those with problems) began asking these very ordinary people all the questions that had been taboo, and found that they were much more prepared to reveal details of their sex lives and sexual fantasies than had previously been the case. The investigators learned, perhaps surprisingly, that women as well as men could have a rich sex-fantasy life and that many of them happily played and enjoyed sex games. They didn't play as many as their partners would like, perhaps, but they certainly didn't merely lie back and dream of their country. All this may seem obvious now but it was a surprise when it was first discovered.

Nevertheless, the nature of these fantasies and sex games was rather different for men than it was for women. Apart from biological considerations which affect *when* they are particularly arousable, women are more aroused by states of mind and attitudes such as "soft lights, sweet music and a considerate partner." Men, on the other hand, are more often aroused by attributes and activities, such as having their partner dressed in a particular way, or having their partner take a dominant or pseudobrutal role during sex. This is one of the reasons why sexual variations are almost exclusively associated with men rather than with women; it is rather easier to describe or practice a behavior than it is an attitude or a mood.

Actually, some variations are biased, either by their nature or by society's attitude toward them, toward being exclusively male-oriented. For example, transvestism—wearing the clothes of the opposite sex—is almost exclusively treated as a male sex deviation because a woman who dresses as a man is both by law and by society's conventions allowed to do so without recrimination, whereas a man who goes out dressed as a woman will almost certainly suffer public scorn. Similarly, although it is possible for a woman to force a man into having intercourse with her, the word "rape" is always used to describe the reverse process, since few men are given to complaining about female assertiveness. Lastly, it is not too flippant to point out that society's attitude towards certain circumstances of nudity is summed up by the comment that a man looking at a nude woman is a voyeur, but a woman looking at a naked man is watching an exhibitionist.

The greater willingness of people to speak of their sex lives and the increase of far more explicit sexy books available on the open market showed that, while a great deal of interest and activity was centered on the sex act itself, three variations were beginning to stand out from the rest, either because of their greater popularity (as variations go) or because they were easier to talk about than other more recherché behaviors. These three variations are the subject matter of this book.

The first variation takes the form of a pattern in which the dominant and submissive accompaniments of lovemaking are separated, stylized and explored—an interest that has produced a host of porn magazines which hardly seem to warrant the older images conjured up by the term "sadomasochism." True, the more brutal aspects of this variation do not seem to be very far behind in these magazines; a casual stroll through the most respectable sex shops reveals many representations of arrogant young ladies flourishing canes, whips and other instruments of undoubted efficiency. Somehow, though, most of the general public seem to have treated these excesses with some irreverence: although they have reacted strongly against those who would legalize sex with children, and even now have a considerable ambivalence towards homosexuality, they have made sadomasochism the subject of jokes, accepted it with a casual shrug, treated those who enjoy its practices with the sort of tolerant bemusedness reserved for the slightly mad or simply ignored it.

The second variation, fetishism, seems to be suffering the same sort of fate. Fetishism can be defined as a condition wherein certain parts of the body, fabrics, articles of clothing or other inanimate objects become in themselves a focus of sexual attraction. It has of course been in existence since time immemorial, but the public has in recent years become more aware of its potential by the exotic creations of free-wheeling fashion designers and underwear manufacturers, coupled with the development of the general idea that the occasional addition of a sexy costume as a sauce to the main dish of lovemaking is socially acceptable.

Once more there is a bias toward the variation being more a male preserve, for, quite apart from any other reason, women are allowed by society not only to place any fabric they like next to their bodies but to display such fabrics openly as well.

Silk, satin, velvet, fur, leather, rubber and plastic are all fetish fabrics that are often part of female clothing. Only leather is permitted to the male, or perhaps fur trimmings if these are kept modestly short. The "peach out of reach" may help at least to maintain the sexual excitant value of a fabric to those males who wish to wear the fetish material.

The two above-mentioned sexual variations (fetishism and low-level sadomasochism) were fused into a powerful yet socially acceptable formula when the original *Avengers* series thundered across television screens in the mid-sixties. The fact that its aggressive, leather-clad heroine, Cathy Gale, wore a *green* cat-suit in which to tangle ritualistically with whatever improbable villains were created each week was irrelevant to the millions who watched her black-and-white screen progress. "Kinky black leather" became a conversational joke and Cathy Gale's outfits vied with the doings of governments for media attention. Thus fetishism—with or without that label —came very much out into the open.

Transvestism, on the other hand, has not "come out" in the same way. As we said, a woman is allowed by society to dress in male clothes but seldom intends that society should take her for a man. In fact, she can actually enhance her female appearance by dressing in this fashion. A man, however, hardly enhances his virility by wearing a dress—usually he looks absurd. If, on the other hand, he makes his disguise complete by means of wig, makeup and other female accoutrements, the consequences upon detection can be very unpleasant for him.

This factor alone does not explain why transvestism appears to be so much of a secretive behavior. There are far fewer sexy books featuring transvestism than there are devoted to sadomasochism and fetishism. This could be due to a lower incidence of this variation in the general population, or to the fact that transvestites are shyer about their predilection, even in relation to those who would supply their needs in magazine form. A more powerful reason for the secrecy, however, is its less attractive display even in private; whereas fetishistic or sadomasochistic presentation can be attractive (or at least not actively off-putting) to a partner, the costumed transvestite can seldom avoid presenting himself in an unattractive light to even an understanding partner. As one interviewee put it, "if a leather freak dresses in some of his gear and shows himself to his girl he may look a bit unusual, or even sinister, but that is all. On the other hand, if a TV puts on what he wants to and parades himself to anyone he values, then ten to one he just looks damn stupid."

The transvestite is thus caught in the trap where, if his transformation is effective, he destroys his masculinity (which hardly enhances him to his partner), while if it is not, he looks ridiculous. His sexual outlet may take place either with a woman who for reasons best known to herself will praise his female appearance, however imperfect, or with a male companion who shares his predilection and who will, with rather more honesty, assist his feminization with both praise and constructive criticism. But both these outlets are rare; far more often his sexual expression will be realized alone, in front of a mirror which provides a sexual "partner" in the form of the transvestite's idealized image.

This, then, is the status today of these three variations. Few books of factual information on the subject exist, and the attitude of the general public cannot help but be biased by the sensational treatment often given to such sexual variations in the media. For devotees of any of these variations, there is of course a lot of "literature" available, but little of it contains information beyond a sort of verbal massage which accompanies its titillatory purpose. Most of it is written by members of the group that is likely to read it—transvestites writing for transvestites, fetishists writing for fetishists and so on. Although by the law of averages a few of these writers might be psychologists, it would appear that apart from the surveys of sexual behavior, most of the writing puts forward introspectively derived and untested theories, often presented in an *ex cathedra* way which can easily persuade the reader to accept them as proven fact rather than as plausible speculation.

There are, nevertheless, two books at least which have made a serious attempt to present more facts than theories. The first is Gillian Freeman's book, *The Undergrowth of Literature*, which presents a survey of the behavior and the literature associated in particular with sexual variation. The book concludes with a masterly presentation of the similarity between children's cartoon characters such as Batman and Robin, Wonder Woman and Snow White's wicked stepmother, and the archetypal figures of pornographic fantasy.

The second book perhaps demands rather more attention, for it is an inadvertent model of both the strengths and weaknesses which have until recently typified and limited any attempt to write a serious book on this type of subject, oriented toward a general rather than specialized readership. The book in question is *The Outer Fringe of Sex*, written by Dr. Maurice North. It is a popularized and inadvertently titillating account of just one fetish—rubber—and its frequent accompaniment, bondage. In a way, the book was at the time of publication something of a milestone, for it set out in quite extraordinary detail the behavior, the reading matter and the historical and social background of those who find pleasure in this variation. It also contained a small number of sadly incomplete case histories—incomplete in that they gave little information about the interviewees beyond their predilection. Somewhat to the amazement of its publishers, it sold over twenty thousand copies in hardcover alone, and the highly successful paperback edition is still selling steadily. The hardcover sales figure, let it be said, is four times higher than anyone suspected would be sold.

In retrospect, however, such a sale is not unexpected, for the incidence of this type of fetishism is now thought to be far higher than the original figure of about 0.1 percent of the population. No reliable estimate of its popularity exists even now, but demand for garments made of this material (which do not feature in conventional fashion at all, remember) is sufficient to support the activities of numerous suppliers in the United States. It is nevertheless not disloyal to Dr. North to say that the book suffers from the same fatal weakness that has until recently dogged all earlier research in this field: it dealt *and could only deal with* such people who, even under the cloak of anonymity, could be contacted and would come forward to speak of their feelings and behavior. These people seem in the light of more recent surveys to have presented rather extreme viewpoints, and may even have presented their deeper fantasies as reality; as a result, the book set forth in surprising detail the repetitive fantasies and eulogies of its practitioners, and thus inadvertently put off a number of the partners of those who enjoyed the material as a sexual sauce (rather than as a total sexual focus) when those partners read the book in an endeavor at least to understand the phenomenon. Only too easily did such readers forget that its title of *The* Outer *Fringe of Sex* was true in two senses.

It is perhaps too much to hope that the present volume will entirely correct the deficiencies inherent in the work of Dr. North, and the rather distorted impressions thereby created. Even now it cannot be said that everything about the how, why and wherefore of the development and practice of sexual variation is by any means known. But from many areas of psychology and sociology, clues, snippets of information, controlled experiments and, above all, the greater willingness of people to reveal to sympathetic investigators the intimacies of fact and fantasy in their sexual lives, a spider's-web of evidence concerning these fascinating phenomena has begun to be drawn together. In some places and at certain times sexual variation may seem natural; in others it may seem sinister. It is our hope that we have set the work of previous writers in a wider and more natural context.

There is a moral problem in the area of sexual variation which must be mentioned before we move on to the results of our investigations. Any book that purports to examine questions of sexual behavior runs into an unavoidable difficulty. Sexuality is fenced in by taboos, beliefs and judgments which are not always based on fact but on feelings. It is thus practically inevitable that there will be a number of people who in all sincerity regard even the discussion of the subject of sexual variation as undesirable. With equal sincerity, we cannot regard such a view as tenable. Our researches lead us to believe that the subject is a fit one for examination, for we are not necessarily defending a viewpoint. If we find that, for example, fetishists are no less masculine in their attitudes towards sex than anyone else, we could argue that they *might* be regarded as more acceptable to society than seems to be the case, but not that they *should* be so regarded. Again, it may be pointless to argue that because millions of girlie magazines are bought every month, the practice should be regarded as normal and acceptable, for the moralist may justifiably feel that although the practice may be popular, it is still morally wrong.

We nevertheless do have some sympathy with the moralistic attitude, for we are aware that, as David Holbrook has pointed out in his book, *Sex and Dehumanisation,* the scientific approach can induce a mechanistic attitude which can interfere with the love-and-emotion component accompanying happy sex. In the hundreds of contacts that we have had with those who find a particular sex idea attractive, we have noticed a dualistic attitude. It doesn't appear in all our interviewees, but it does in many of them, and takes the form of a certain defensiveness towards the behavior in question. The moralist might say that this arises from an awareness that what they (the practitioners) are doing is wrong. The sociologist, on the other hand, would reply that the defensiveness stems from the pressure generated within the individual because he thinks that society rejects his behavior. We clearly cannot profit by becoming too involved in this argument. We can only conclude that if such behavior is in any way felt to be a problem, then a fuller knowledge of the facts and studies pertaining to the subject will be beneficial to those who for any reason—medical, social, moral, psychological or personal—are involved.

1

Who, and What, Is Normal?

The special research that has gone into the preparation of this book has been done over a period of about three years. It has entailed conversations and interviews not only with clinicians, crisis-intervention groups, counselors and others whose job it is to help those whose sex lives have definitely gone awry, but also with the far greater number of people who have answered questionnaires, provided case histories or simply emptied their hearts to us in an endeavor to describe and explain their behavior, feelings and thoughts. Some had no particular axe to grind in doing so; some did so in an effort to save others from the opprobrium that had affected their lives, and others in the hope of bringing about a more liberal attitude toward their own behavior. Yet over and over again, one question has been raised, perhaps in a hundred ways, but always to the same end: namely, whether they or their activities and fantasies were "normal." Let it be said at once that the question is not, and is never likely to be, answerable by a straight yes or no, for the word "normal" has at least three meanings which must be separated before any answer can be attempted.

The first definition is the statistical one, and can be most simply described by means of an example. If we take a large number of people from as wide a variety of sources as possible, and measure the height of each one, then we find that the very tall and the very short are in the minority. By far the greatest number lies in the intermediate range, and so in a sense it is *less* normal to be over six feet tall or under five feet tall than it is to be five four or five eight. But at what point do we say that a person is abnormally tall or short—that his height is abnormal? Any cutoff point is bound to be arbitrary. We could, for example, set the minority level at 5 percent of the total population, so that as far as height is concerned, 2.5 percent could be regarded as abnormally short and another 2.5 percent as abnormally tall.

Notice, however, that the word "normal" is now no longer floating about on its own. One has to say "normal *in terms of height.*" Of course, one can be normal in twenty ways and abnormal in twenty others, making the blanket question "Am I normal?" complete nonsense unless a particular attribute is specified.

However, when one of the subjects of this book asks "Am I normal?" he generally means "Is the particular behavior or way of thinking that puts me into the group you are studying normal?" Yet even when we use the arbitrary cutoff method, we run into another problem. What criterion do we use for putting that person into that particular group? One might assume that the person is either a fetishist (or a sadomasochist or a transvestite) or he isn't. That's what some workers—especially in the therapy area—used to think. After all, they argued, if a man turns up at the clinic and says that he's a fetishist, then he should know, and we can start from there.

Unfortunately, the moment you step outside the clinic you find that it isn't as simple as that. Kinsey's *Report on the Sexual Behavior of the Human Male,* published in 1948, showed this with respect to homosexuality. Look at the following arrangement of findings based on a sample of 5,300 American males, and try to decide how many of these men could formally be classified as homosexual.

1. Thirty-seven percent of men have experienced homosexual orgasm at some time after puberty.
2. An additional 13 percent have felt homosexual urges without acting upon them.
3. Twenty-five percent of men have more than incidental homosexual experiences between the ages of sixteen and fifty-five.
4. Eighteen percent of men have at least as much homosexual as heterosexual experience during at least one three-year period between the ages of sixteen and fifty-five.
5. Ten percent are almost exclusively homosexual for at least three years between the ages of sixteen and fifty-five.
6. Four percent are exclusively homosexual throughout their lives after puberty.

Clearly, there is no simple answer to the question of whether or not a man is "abnormal." Our studies of people who find rubber sexually exciting reveal that many such people enjoy a conventional sexual relationship with their regular partners on certain occasions, while at other times enjoying activities which center around rubber with the same partner, a different partner or by themselves. Are such people to be classified as fetishists or not?

One way to get around this problem—and the one which has been used extensively in providing data for this book—is to use rating scales. For example, a question such as "How frequently do you have fantasies about activity X?" is asked, and the person concerned is asked to check one of the following categories:

Never　　　　(score 0)
Seldom　　　 (score 1)
Occasionally　(score 2)
Sometimes　　(score 3)

Often   (score 4)
Regularly   (score 5)

As we shall see, groups who have admitted being "into" activity X have higher average scores than groups who have not. On this evidence we could say that an individual whose score is unusually high on this scale, say in the top 2.5 percent of people, is "abnormal," though we doubt that much would be gained by applying the term in this way.

The main advantage of this definition of abnormality is that it does not necessarily carry moral overtones. One can with this criterion happily fall in the minority without feeling guilty about it, no more than one need feel guilty about being a fanatical chess-player (for the latter group also comprises less than 2.5 percent of the population).

Before moving on to other ideas about what is meant by "normal" we might consider one possible criticism of our rating scale, that not everyone has the same idea of how often is "often" (score 4) or "occasionally" (score 2), and so on. Each person's concept of the actual frequencies involved may be different. Studies have shown that, where a large number of estimates are made, a good average consensus on these frequencies does emerge. This is fine when making generalizations about group scores, but it does call into question the validity of an individual score. When a subject comes along, score card in hand, and asks "Am I normal?" he might just be the man for whom "often" is once a month instead of the consensus for that question of once a day. (Filmgoers may remember the scene in *Annie Hall* in which Woody Allen, asked by a marriage counselor how often he and Annie have sex, replies "Hardly ever—I'd say only about three times a week." Independently asked the same question, Annie replies "All the time, doctor—at least three times a week.") And what makes things even more tricky is that the statistics we used often assume that the difference between "regularly" (score 5) and "often" (score 4) is the same as that between "often" and "sometimes" (score 3), and so on down the line.

Fortunately, though, it turns out that when people are given a questionnaire in which a fair number of questions of this nature are posed and the respondents use the same rating scale for answering each question, they end up making a scale for themselves in which the intervals *are* just about equal even if the original concepts of "seldom," "sometimes" and "often" are quietly forgotten.

Of course, a hard-nosed scientist might argue that a question concerning fantasies, such as the one above, is highly dubious anyway because one man's idle thought may be another's seething desire. Perhaps, therefore, it would be better to observe the behavior concerned by rephrasing the question: "How often do you *carry out* this activity X?" There are times when this is assuredly the preferable approach; but not always, for there are many reasons why people might not dream of attempting to carry out their fantasies. One person we interviewed had very frequent and intense fantasies of being whipped unmercifully by an Amazonian woman dressed in a spectacular costume made up of myriads of tiny lit-up electric bulbs. He had, however, never put this fantasy into practice, even though the fantasy, the financial means and the social opportunity had been with him for a number of years. Why not? Because if the woman didn't do her stuff properly, it wouldn't live up to his fantasy, while if she did, it would almost kill him! It was not because he could not get an obliging professional to perform the service; it was not because the costume was too bizarre to have made—it was simply because he wasn't up to it physiologically.

To some extent, fantasy and practice go hand in hand. In the case of the "rubberites" mentioned earlier, 90 percent scored "abnormally" high on scales of both fantasy and activity connected with rubber. The connection is not absolute, however, and this poses a problem. Freud defined a fetishist as someone for whom erotic arousal was impossible unless the fetish object was present. However, he never made clear whether the fetish object had to be *physically* present or whether its mental presence is sufficient. We said earlier that the rubberites could on some occasions have a conventional relationship—in terms of activity—with their regular partner. This would preclude them from being fetishists in Freud's terms, for rubber would not be physically in evidence. However, we have no idea what these people were fantasizing about while the "conventional relationship" was going on.

Mention of Dr. Freud brings us to the second definition of normality, which is medically or pathologically oriented. At first, this definition equated "healthy" with "normal" and "sick" with "abnormal." Historically, this definition worked well with physical illnesses because, in spite of temporary situations like an outbreak of plague, most people had a reasonable idea of how a healthy person looked, felt and behaved, and knew that most people were physically healthy most of the time. Physical ailments were also found to have definite physical causes, many had remedies to combat them and one could often predict what would happen to the patient if he didn't avail himself of those remedies.

Mental disorders complicated the picture somewhat, for the symptoms, causes and remedies were far less clear. For centuries some authorities avoided the issue by labeling certain of these mental aberrations as "works of the Devil" (or, occasionally, of the Almighty), thus passing the responsibility to someone else. Even today, the dilemma persists in that many psychological anomalies have no known cause, in the sense that a virus can be identified as a cause, no agreed-upon method of treatment and no uniquely predictable outcome.

Even serious conditions like schizophrenia turn out to have no single cause but a multiplicity of symptoms, no omnipotent method of treatment but a highly variable response to treatment. This has led some psychiatrists, such as R. D. Laing, to throw overboard the whole concept of schizophrenia as a disease in the medical sense, and to rationalize the symptoms as a logical set of thoughts and actions arising in response to the irrational and intolerable way of life that has been thrust upon the patient by his environment. This idea, however, is as yet unproven.

And in the world of sex, things are in a way more curious still. Unusual sex patterns and predilections can be found in anyone—young or old, rich or poor, male or female. What is more, they can be found in people who otherwise don't feel themselves to be "sick" or "abnormal" in any way. It is thus doubly difficult in this field to equate "unhealthy" with "abnormal" with any degree of confidence. During our researches we came across considerable numbers of people who, while having a predilection for one or more of the sexual variations explored in this book, expressed no wish to be "cured" of that predilection. A survey of the club whose 400 members enjoy "sadomasochistic" fantasies and activities indicated that only 15 percent of the membership wished to be relieved of their propensity: an interestingly low figure.

It seems, then, that no definition of abnormality in terms of "illness" is meaningful in this domain, and it is encouraging to note that many clinicians have begun to adopt the more sensible view that only if a person is unhappy about his state should he be regarded as a suitable case for treatment. But medical traditions die hard, and the idea of *a* cause, *a* cure and so on often carries over into the clinician's attitude. Sometimes there may be a contributing physiological factor. Later on we will consider evidence that fetishism and transvestism may be associated with small lesions or scars in the brain tissue, but this sort of influence does seem to be minor; the greater bulk of evidence indicates that our sexual behavior, conventional or otherwise, is shaped by experiences in childhood or adolescence which propel us inexorably and "logically" in the direction of whatever turns us on. We use the word "logically" because, although it may not seem logical to anyone outside the group in question to derive sexual arousal from fantasizing over, say, spanking a schoolgirl's backside, the particular set of events experienced by the person in question make it virtually inevitable that such a connection will occur. These learning experiences are not at first entered into deliberately, although later on they may be selected in order to confirm what the growing mind has come to believe. This strengthens the link between situation and response, and the die is very soon cast.

The moralist may of course point out that because X is logical or inevitable, it is not necessarily right, and this leads to the third way of looking at normality and abnormality. Psychologist George Kelly says that guilt is the emotion we experience when we notice that our feelings or behavior do not match up with how we think we ought to feel or behave. Generally, guilt occurs when we evaluate our feelings and actions as being in some way atypical and inferior to those of the society around us.

Now, as we have said, what we actually feel and do is perfectly logical to us, because our feelings and actions are virtually inevitable. What we think we *ought* to do and feel, on the other hand, is derived largely from our appraisal of other people's feelings and actions—either generally, in the form of "what the world says," or specifically, in the form of "what my mom/dad/partner says." In such terms, a person generally judges himself as abnormal if he considers his feelings and behavior at variance with his views of what the world thinks. This is usually an easy criterion to follow because we can often get a very good idea of the norms of society by asking people and observing their behavior. We *know* as we grow up that it is normal to feel murderously inclined toward some people at times, but that it is not normal to murder them in reality.

When it comes to sex, however, the taboos that for good or evil surround the subject make finding out rather more difficult. We can't easily ask our friends whether they enjoy secretly dressing in their wife's clothes. Because of these taboos about "finding out," beliefs and facts can be at considerable variance. One of the most surprising things that emerged from the previously cited Kinsey report, and its companion volume on the sexual behavior of women, was the unexpectedly high incidence of adult masturbation and the popularity of oral sex among both men and women. Everyone had previously believed that few other people did it and that most frowned on it, so that if they themselves did it, they were abnormal. Then Kinsey proved that a lot of people did it, so maybe it wasn't abnormal after all.

This is why many people who enjoy particular sexual activities and feelings come back to the idea of "whatever I want to do is all right as long as I don't upset anyone else." We neither wish to attack nor defend this view, because it can be either valid or invalid, helpful or detrimental. We have known of couples who, on finding by virtue of their past learning experiences that conventional channels of sexual communication are inefficient, have developed alternative, less conventional, patterns which have given them a satisfaction they could never otherwise have achieved. On the other hand, the man who obtains greater satisfaction by masturbating while fantasizing about a situation that in practice would be intolerable to his wife, might come to prefer that activity to conventional lovemaking and thus deprive his wife of sexual fulfillment.

So far it seems that we have paid little respect to the virtues of love, of caring, of affection. Intuitively, however, we feel that modern society possesses an extra, almost unspoken, criterion of normality which transcends the definitions that we have put forth so far. This definition may be idealistic and difficult to utilize, but it is well worth bearing in mind as a desirable end. It is simply this: "That which promotes love, caring and affection between people is normal; that which divides them is abnormal."

2

The People Studied, the Methods Used

In the opening chapter it was suggested that only a few of those who enjoy the type of variations discussed in this book ever feel under enough pressure about their leanings to seek medical or other professional help to enable them to cope with that pressure. Interviews with members of each group have convinced us that most of them just continue doing what they enjoy, deriving a great deal of fun out of it and regarding it as "just one of those things." Others may feel pressured, shy, guilty or upset about it, but they, too, salvage what pleasure they can out of their state and shrug off their hangups as best they can. Clearly, any complete study of sexual variations must utilize this overall group, and not rely solely upon samples appearing in psychiatric clinics.

Contacting this silent majority is another matter. One can advertise for, say, left-handed people or women bringing up children alone, asking them to come and help with some psychological research, and hope to get a reasonable response. Similar requests addressed to men who are turned on by submitting to the attentions of Miss Whiplash, or by dressing in leather garments, yield virtually no response at all. Such individuals are, understandably, not given to proclaiming the fact openly.

However, there are now clubs and societies catering to the interests of devotees of these variations. Their members sometimes meet, more often correspond, and certainly take comfort from the fact that there are many other people with tendencies similar to their own. We have drawn much of our data from these societies, contacting the secretary of each group and asking permission for our questionnaires to be sent out to every member. Sometimes we corresponded at great length. Sometimes we attended meetings and social events run by the clubs.

Incidentally, these meetings are not the orgies of unrestrained lust one might imagine; they are more likely to be a barbecue, a dinner/dance or a visit to the theater, with little to distinguish the group from any other, except perhaps the particular self-mocking in-jokes that typify any minority group or, possibly, the clothes that they wear. Transvestites usually remain in male clothes in public, and if their cross-dressed appearance is unbecoming to their image. If, however, they pass easily as women, they may do so and the chances are that nobody will notice because they won't be looking in the first place. In private, on the other hand, there is certain to be a prevalence of feminine attire, but about as much sexuality as there is at a meeting of the local Junior League. Fetishists can afford to be a little more obvious; we have attended a dinner/dance of a fetishistic group in a large London hotel where some of the wives or girlfriends of the members displayed fairly exotic and, to the tastes of many people, attractive outfits featuring their partner's favorite material. Interestingly, it was neither the members nor their ladies who appeared uncomfortable as they moved through the foyer to their suite; if anything, it was the other hotel guests who looked distressed. Sadomasochists, meanwhile, have no such "public appearance" problem. Masters or mistresses leading slaves about on a collar and chain in public are largely creations of pornographic fantasy.

The type of person who joins a club may, however, be slightly different from the type that does not, so we extended our net further by leaving our questionnaire sets in appropriate book stores, boutiques and sex shops. As our work proceeded, we also received and took up offers to distribute our material overseas. As a result, we believe that while our sample might not be totally representative of the world's sadomasochists, fetishists and transvestites, it is at least more comprehensive than would have been the case had we relied exclusively on clinical sources.

The willingness to help of both the subjects who provided data and of those who distributed our material was most gratifying. And, paradoxically, this cooperation was much more difficult to obtain from people whose sexual patterns were conventional. The so-called "normals," with whom our variant groups were to be compared, were far more suspicious of our attempts to obtain data from them than were the variant subjects. To some readers this may come as no surprise, since invasion of privacy can be felt by all of us, and our special groups were at least encouraged to trust us by means of a message from club officials. However, since the questionnaires were totally anonymous, could be filled in at leisure and came with a letter of introduction explaining the scientific nature of our research, one might have anticipated an equal willingness on the part of the general public. As it was, we could not help but notice how much more difficult it was to obtain data from the "normals" to complete our age-matched control sample than to obtain data from the special groups. In the end, we found the departure lounges of airports to be a particularly fruitful source of people who could be persuaded to help, thus enabling us to match for age and social class more or less as required.

Of course, most people do tend to be shy about revealing details of their sex lives, so can we assume that, when they do answer questions, they are telling the truth? We can never be entirely sure, because even with the best will in the world, people vary in their responses to the same question asked at two different times. However, anonymity helps to promote honesty, and since, on returning their questionnaires, two-thirds of our subjects attached their names and addresses so that, if we wished, we could return to them to ask further questions, we were able to carry out follow-up interviews, excerpts from which are reported in this book. In the course of these interviews, we were able to do a certain amount of discreet cross-checking. The opportunity was taken to allow some of the interviewees to look through their questionnaires and in no instance was any answer changed as a result. This was a very encouraging discovery, though admittedly, it might only mean that if someone wished to lie, then at least he lied consistently! Nevertheless, we got the impression during our investigations that the majority of those in the variant groups were only too eager to learn the truth about their "type" of person, and it seems logical that neither they nor we had much to gain by deliberately falsifying information.

The societies or clubs from which we obtained data are various in nature and organization. The rubber-fetishist data was obtained largely from members of the discreetly named Mackintosh Society, an England-based group with members in no less than twenty-three countries. A liking for mackintoshes—rubberized raincoats—is, of course, only one form of rubber fetish. The name may have been deliberately chosen for its ambiguity and the possibility of more respectable interpretations. One meeting of the Society we attended was held on the premises of a famous and rather conservative club; from the attitudes of the staff we wondered if those who accepted the booking had been expecting a reunion of the Clan Mackintosh rather than the company that actually appeared. The membership of the society has passed the 1,000 mark, of which just over half are active in attending meetings or entering into two-way correspondence. Eighty-seven members of this society answered our questionnaires and about one-third of these were interviewed in addition.

The Mackintosh Society exists partly as a social club and

partly as a self-help organization with the particular function
of reassuring those who are puzzled, embarrassed or isolated
as a result of their sexual predilection that there are others in
the same boat. It publishes a rather innocuous quarterly magazine which contains reports of meetings; occasional pictures
of women (who are sometimes members' wives or girlfriends)
wearing various styles of rainwear; self-mocking cartoons and
nostalgic reminiscences, in prose or verse, of the days when
the particular visual, tactile, aural and olfactory qualities of
rubberized rainwear could, without difficulty, be appreciated
by the devotee. The innocuousness of this organ may in part
be conditioned by the Society's view that wives and girlfriends should at least know about their man's bent even if
they do not wish to please him by wearing garments made of
rubber. Such an acceptance might well be jeopardized by the
presentation of some of the more extreme rubberite activities.

This difficulty of presenting an acceptable image to wives
and the rest of society in the face of the wide range of possible
fetishistic behaviors, arose in a particularly acute form when
two members of the National Film School in Beaconsfield
made a film called *Dressing for Pleasure*. This portrayed the
activities of those who enjoyed putting on garments rather
than taking them off in order to gain sexual pleasure or
arousal. Although the film was made with the cooperation of
the Mackintosh Society, it was not controlled by them in terms
of content. It presented quite a range of fetishistic behavior,
including the semi-occlusive costumes and multi-layer cover-
ages which some fetishists enjoy. As a result, it caused much
controversy among members when shown at a Society meeting, since some would have preferred that the presentation of
the more extreme modes of dress had been omitted so that
wives and girlfriends might not believe these to be the norm
and become less sympathetic to the Society.

Meetings of the Mackintosh Society are fairly frequent, and
take place in many parts of the country. Their format is largely
social—a dinner, a discussion forum, a barbecue, a visit to a
local place of interest, a river trip, a nature walk and so on.

About half of the members, and a few of their partners, wear something in their favorite material, if the locale is appropriate. No doubt they are one of the few social groups who don't mind when it rains on one of their outdoor meetings!

Leather fetishists in England are not so well served, for they have no society that actually meets as a group. Some may claim that since leather is well accepted as a material that can be worn in public, there is no need for such a society. The counter-argument is that while leather is accepted in certain garments, the type of outfit the true leatherite loves would cause more of a stir in public. (Advocates recently tested this suggestion by having an agreeable young lady walk down a busy London street dressed in a tight leather jumpsuit and spike-heeled boots. Nobody actually complained, but the number of people walking into lampposts or nearly driving into the car ahead proved the point adequately.)

In the absence of an appropriate society, our leatherite group was drawn from members of a correspondence club run by the owner of Atomage, a London-based company which makes high-quality specialized garments in leather and vinyl. The term "specialized" in this case covers theatrical and operatic costumes as well as erotic wear.

Atomage publishes two magazines devoted to fetishism. One of these is sold on the open market and acts as, among other things, a publicity vehicle for the company's more conventional garments. The second goes only to members of the correspondence club and contains material on occlusive and restrictive themes which are extremely exciting to those who are fetishistically and sadomasochistically inclined. To those who are more conventionally inclined the material is likely to be incomprehensible. The correspondence club is no more than that; Atomage's owner seldom introduces members to one another, except perhaps socially when they meet by chance in his showroom. Inevitably, though, he is the repository of many of his clients' personal and sexual secrets.

The correspondence club has about 200 members, but those seventy who lived in the United Kingdom and who could be subsequently interviewed were contacted for the purposes of our research. Thirty-eight of these returned questionnaires. With this group, we were able to estimate to what extent leatherites were attracted to other materials. Although the average rating for erotic interest in rubber was just as high as it was for leather (eight out of ten on a rating scale, with vinyl scoring less than four points), there was a tendency for a strong liking for one material to correlate with lower ratings for the other. Because of this, rubberites from the Mackintosh Society and leatherites from Atomage's correspondence club have been analyzed as separate groups. Data to be discussed later show this to have been a reasonable decision. While there are very many similarities between the groups, there are occasional differences which are of theoretical interest.

Our sadomasochistic group was obtained through "Cooperative Motivational Research," a correspondence club which caters exclusively to sadomasochists, providing members with a means of communication. At the same time it carries out some basic statistical and sociological research on its members in order to better understand the phenomenon of sadomasochism. The club issues a quarterly journal which carries not only general articles, testimonies, fantasies and personal ads that solicit partners, but also informed articles on the subject of sadomasochism, written by doctors and psychologists. Most of these contributions are theoretical or speculative, but more objective data, derived internally from the group, has been obtained by the club secretary, who periodically sends out questionnaires with the club magazine for members to fill in. Some of the findings from the club's own research program will be reported later in the book along with our own data. Our questionnaires were sent to all 600 or so members, and 133 of them contributed data to our research.

Transvestites, and the small group of transsexuals studied in Chapter 7, were contacted with the help of the Beaumont Society, which caters exclusively to these two groups. The Society became independent from an American group, the Foundation for Full Personality Expression, in 1966, although it retains an affiliation with it. According to its introductory leaflet, the Beaumont Society is "dedicated to providing transvestites with a means of self-acceptance, peace of mind and understanding, in place of loneliness, fear and self-condemnation"—an aim which corresponds fairly well with those of the other groups we have studied. The Society operates a contact system allowing members to get to know each other by letter, and holds both national and regional meetings.

There is also a counseling service designed to help the transvestite's partner gain a better understanding of her man's situation. Help is offered both by the wives of transvestites and professional workers who have had experience with the problems faced by transvestites. A bimonthly magazine contains articles and letters contributed by members and provides a forum in which members can participate, as well as a classified shopping guide to places where clothes, wigs, makeup and the like can be bought. Interestingly enough, these are by no means always shops serving only the transvestite or transsexual, but are "open" shops where a membership card will ensure sympathetic treatment from a member of the staff who is knowledgeable about the needs of a Beaumont customer. Two hundred and sixty-nine Beaumont Society members provided us with data.

The last group, to be dealt with in Chapter 7, consists of women who advertise in sadomasochistically oriented sex magazines, particularly one published in London called *Superbitch*. By no means must it be thought that these women are all professionals, in this market only for money; some are simply eager to enjoy themselves in the particular sex game that turns them on. Even more interesting is the discovery that those who are professionals also frequently enjoy what they do and obtain direct sexual arousal out of their "sessions" with a client. As one such lady told us, " 'Straight' girls in our game are often bored out of their minds with a john, and in any case they are not going to be with him long. My customers have two-hour sessions with me, and I have to think, interact, know their special likes and be creative. And any woman will tell you that interaction—plus affection if you're lucky—makes it easier to turn on." Women of this type—whether professional or not—are nevertheless not easy to find and not always eager to help with research. Despite cooperation from the editor of *Superbitch* in tracing women of this calling, we were able to obtain data from only twenty-five contacts.

It may be useful at this point to summarize the details of our subject samples. Listed in the table below are the numbers of people in each group who provided us with quantifiable questionnaire data. The average age for each group is also provided. All of these subjects were male except for the "superbitches," and of course some of the transsexuals who had begun as males but were now well on their way to being female, if they had not already achieved this status. These subjects completed two questionnaires, one to assess personality characteristics and the other designed to examine sexual fantasies and behavior and to elicit statistical details such as age, marital status, occupation, upbringing and sexual history.

The personality test used was the *Eysenck Personality Questionnaire,* published by Professor Hans Eysenck and Dr. Sybil Eysenck in 1975. The Eysencks' work in defining and isolating three major personality variables is so fundamental that it seemed to us useful to use this questionnaire rather than any other which might give us more information by asking many more questions but might also put off a lot of respondents by the time it took to fill in. The questionnaire measures three aspects of personality, namely extraversion, neuroticism and psychoticism. It also includes a "lie scale" which is intended to provide a check on the candidness of response. Since the psychological usage of these terms differs slightly from what is generally understood by them, we have included brief definitions.

Extraversion, a mixture of sociability, outgoingness and impulsiveness, is probably the personality variable that is best understood by people. The typical extravert likes going to parties and enjoys talking to people; he is inclined to play

Summary of subject samples

Name of group	Activity or preference	No. of subjects	Mean age	Age variation (Standard deviation)
Mackintosh Society	Rubber fetishism	87	45.5	10.0
Atomage correspondence club	Leather fetishism	38	44.3	11.0
Cooperative Motivation Research	Sadomasochism	133	44.7	12.2
Beaumont Society	Transvestism	269	41.9	12.7
	Transsexualism	16	43.8	11.5
Normal men	Nonspecific	50	43.9	10.1
Superbitches	Dominant women	25	33.7	8.9
Normal women	Nonspecific	25	32.0	9.5

practical jokes, take risks, keep moving and be the life and soul of the party. When things don't go his way, he is easily angered, though a lot of that aggression is merely blowing off steam and is quickly dispersed. By contrast, the introvert, the person who is low on the extraversion scale, is a quiet, studious person, happy to be on his own, liking to have "a place for everything, and everything in its place." He keeps his feelings well under control, is reliable and often has high moral or ethical standards.

Neuroticism is one of those unfortunate words that gets used for a wide variety of things—generally quite inappropriately. A better word would be "emotionality." The person who is high on the neuroticism scale is, in short, a worrier. He is often moody, sleeps badly, overreacts to stresses and suffers from minor, vague illnesses which others suspect to be "all in the mind." Sometimes, however, he can turn this emotionality to advantage, since he is often quite sensitive to the emotions and moods of others. The "stable" person, who is low on the neuroticism scale, is the opposite of all this, being calm, even-tempered, controlled and unworried. This is usually a good thing but, of course, it may mean he is a little insensitive, a little dull, a little unresponsive.

Psychoticism is a rather frightening word but, curiously enough, encompasses qualities that we can admire at times because of their effectiveness in getting certain things done. Those who are high on the psychoticism scale tend to be tough, aggressive, manipulative and cold, occasionally to the extent of being antisocial and bizarre in their behavior. The term "psychoticism" was first used because the Eysencks found that mental patients diagnosed as schizophrenic, paranoid and manic tended to score high on the scale. However, it is clearly an incomplete description because psychopaths and criminals—particularly those convicted of violent crimes—score just as high as psychotic patients, if not higher. Where normal levels of psychoticism are concerned, the term "tough-mindedness" is probably a better description of this personality dimension. The trait is of particular relevance to the present research because it is closely related to the concept of masculinity. Men score on average higher than women, an observation that has led some theorists to suggest that androgen levels, possibly operative during the embryonic development of the individual, are the biological basis of this personality trait. Low scorers on the psychoticism scale are of course warm, gentle and feminine in their attitudes and behavior.

A great deal of research has gone into establishing these three personality dimensions as "primaries," rather in the sense that red, blue and yellow are primary colors. Just as any color can be made by an appropriate mixture of these three, and in fact is done so every night on color television screens, so the Eysencks believe that the personality of an individual, however unique it might appear, can be fairly well specified by reference to these three independent axes. The items used to score each of them have been carefully selected as "sharp" indicators of these dimensions. Unfortunately, for copyright reasons, it is not possible to reproduce the whole *Eysenck Personality Questionnaire* here, but we have listed below a few sample items from each of the three dimensions to give an idea of how the test is constructed.

Examples of the type of item in the Eysenck Personality Inventory
Are you a very talkative person?
Would you enjoy a lively party?
Do you like plenty of excitement going on around you?
Do you often do things on the spur of the moment?

Are you worried by awful things that might happen?
Do you suffer from "nerves"?
Are you often tired and listless for no good reason?
Would you describe yourself as "moody"?

Would you take drugs that have strange effects on you?
Do you think insurance schemes are a waste of time?
Did you tend to dislike your parents?
Do you sometimes tease animals?

Note: The extravert would tend to answer "yes" to the first four items, the neurotic (emotional) person to the second four and individuals high on the psychoticism (tough-mindedness) scale would respond positively to the last four.

The "lie scale" was originally put into the *Eysenck Personality Questionnaire* to test whether the person filling in that questionnaire was doing so truthfully, or was merely ticking the sort of answer that he felt would show him in a good light. Certainly it does this to a point, especially when the questionnaire is administered under conditions where "faking good" is thought to be advantageous—for example, if the test is being done as part of a job selection procedure. However, it is equally certain that the lie scale may also tap factors other than lying. It may, for example, measure our need to give a good impression in general, i.e., our "respectability" or conservatism. It may reflect the degree to which we feel that the world is looking over our shoulder, or our need for social acceptance—both of which are likely to affect the person with a less usual pattern of sexual behavior—or it may possibly denote some degree of social naïveté. We shall be discussing the interpretation of this scale in terms of the results obtained from each of the variant groups as we come to them.

The other test used was the *Wilson Sex Fantasy Questionnaire*, first published in *The Secrets of Sexual Fantasy* (Wilson, 1978). This was used to rate the prevalence of various forms of sexual fantasy and behavior, to study how different themes are related, and to cross-reference the immediate and derived variables with others such as sexual happiness, inhibition, upbringing, age and so on.

Although our original questionnaire (marginally modified and reprinted on the pages following) contained five columns eliciting fantasy and activity ratings for various sexual situations, it was found in the original studies that the similarity between the responses in each column for any one person was high enough to allow "daytime fantasies" to serve as an index for all the other situations when dealing with people with more or less conventional patterns of sexual behavior. When dealing with a variant group, however, the ratings of fantasy (whether "daytime fantasies" or "fantasies during intercourse or masturbation") seem more easily to part company from the ratings of "have done in reality." This is surprising, for while the fairly conventional fantasy of, say, "sex with a known but untried partner" may with sufficient persuasion and opportunity be converted into ecstatic (or disappointed) reality, more unusual fantasies are more difficult to realize in practice. Women who are prepared to be bound and gagged, whipped or spanked, or to make love to a man who is dressed in a wetsuit or women's clothing are hard to locate even if the men with these desires can overcome their guilt and shyness enough to ask.

We also decided to combine ratings from the "daytime fantasies" and the "fantasies during intercourse or masturbation" column, because daytime fantasies not immediately geared to intercourse or masturbation might loom rather larger in the lives of our respondents than in those whose sex lives are conventional. Most of our analyses make use of two scores: "fantasy ratings," the sum of the daytime fantasy and intercourse/masturbation fantasy ratings; and "activity ratings," which are the self-ratings of what the person has done in reality.

The last page of the questionnaire is designed to obtain some background on the life-style and sexual characteristics of the individual. Some of the questions, e.g. age, marital status and occupation, provide essential demographic data. Other questions are concerned with various aspects of sexual activity, libido and satisfaction. Still others are intended to give some picture of the individual's upbringing, for instance restrictiveness vẽrsus permissiveness in the home, and experience of corporal punishment.

At the end of the questionnaire some of the items were varied according to which special interest group was being tested. Thus the transvestites, for example, were asked to what extent they cross-dressed for arousal and to what extent they did so to enjoy female identification. This is recognized as a key question for separating heterosexual or "fetishistic" transvestites from individuals tending in the direction of transsexualism, a distinction to which we shall devote further attention later in the book. The "superbitch" group of sadomasochistically oriented women were asked to what extent they engaged in these practices for pleasure and to what extent professionally. While, as we have said, these options are not necessarily exclusive, the distinction between them needs to be considered in the interpretation of our results.

These, then, were the questionnaires which were answered by our variant groups, as well as by our supposedly "normal" samples. Naturally, it was not possible to be totally comprehensive in collecting data of this sort from large samples for quantified analysis. Also, we would have liked to have been more flexible in varying the selection of questions given to each group and each individual. Unfortunately, such changes would have made numerical analysis and comparisons between groups impossible. We hope that the less structured interviews that we conducted with several of our subjects to some extent offset this deficiency. On the other hand, such material has limitations from the scientific point of view; because of the danger of selectivity in the choice of case material it should be viewed only as illustrative of the points established by properly controlled, empirical means, or at best as impressionistic, in that it rounds out the picture of the complications that abound in any individual case.

FANTASY QUESTIONNAIRE

Please indicate how often you fantasize about the themes below at various times, how often you do them and how often you would like to do them if given the opportunity.

In each column put a number between 0 and 5 to indicate your frequency as follows:

Never=0, Seldom=1, Occasionally=2, Sometimes=3, Often=4, Regularly=5.

	Daytime fantasies	Fantasies during intercourse or masturbation	Dreams while asleep	Have done in reality	Would like to do in reality
1. Making love out of doors in a romantic setting (e.g. field of flowers, beach at night).					
2. Having intercourse with a loved partner.					
3. Intercourse with someone you know but have not had sex with.					
4. Intercourse with an anonymous stranger.					
5. Sex with two other people.					
6. Participating in an orgy.					
7. Being forced to do something.					
8. Forcing someone to do something.					
9. Homosexual activity.					
10. Receiving oral sex.					
11. Giving oral sex.					

12. Watching others have sex.				
13. Sex with an animal.				
14. Whipping or spanking someone.				
15. Being whipped or spanked.				
16. Taking someone's clothes off.				
17. Having your clothes taken off.				
18. Making love elsewhere than bedroom (e.g. kitchen, bathroom).				
19. Being excited by material or clothing (e.g. rubber, leather, underwear).				
20. Hurting a partner.				
21. Being hurt by a partner.				
22. Mate-swapping.				
23. Being aroused by watching someone urinate.				
24. Being tied up.				
25. Tying someone up.				
26. Having incestuous sexual relations.				
27. Exposing yourself provocatively.				
28. Transvestism (wearing clothes of the opposite sex).				

(Continued)

	Daytime fantasies	Fantasies during intercourse or masturbation	Dreams while asleep	Have done in reality	Would like to do in reality
29. Being promiscuous.					
30. Having sex with someone much younger than yourself.					
31. Having sex with someone much older than yourself.					
32. Being much sought after by the opposite sex.					
33. Being seduced as an "innocent."					
34. Seducing an "innocent."					
35. Being embarrassed by failure of sexual performance.					
36. Having sex with someone of different race.					
37. Using objects for stimulation (e.g. vibrators, candles).					
38. Being masturbated to orgasm by a partner.					
39. Looking at obscene pictures or films.					
40. Kissing passionately.					

Please give the number of the single theme from the above list you find most exciting.

(a) In fantasy ....

(b) In reality ....

Do you have a favorite fantasy that we have omitted? (Describe briefly)

....

....

Please answer these questions

1. Marital status ....

2. Do you have a steady partner, whether you are married or not? ....

3. If yes, how satisfied are you with them sexually? (Please underline)

| Not at all satisfied | Not very satisfied | Reasonably satisfied | Very satisfied | Totally satisfied |

4. Overall, how would you rate your sex life?

| Not at all satisfactory | Not very satisfactory | Reasonably satisfactory | Very satisfactory | Totally satisfactory |

5. How many orgasms do you have in an average week?

| 0–1 | 2–3 | 4–5 | 6–7 | 8+ |

6. Overall, how would you rate your sex drive?

| Very low | Lower than average | Average | Above average | Very high |

7. With how many different people have you had intercourse?

| None | 1–2 | 3–10 | 11–50 | 51+ |

8. How would you describe your upbringing as regards matters of sex?

| Very restrictive | Slightly restrictive | Average | Slightly permissive | Very permissive |

9. How inhibited do you think you are sexually?

| Very inhibited | Slightly inhibited | Average | Slightly uninhibited | Very uninhibited |

10. As a child, did you receive corporal punishment either at home or at school?

| Never | Seldom | Sometimes | Often | Regularly |

3

What Do They Do?

Even twenty years ago, people generally did not find it easy
to talk about any form of sex. Nowadays, so long as the activity
is confined to a pattern which society has somehow agreed is
acceptable, they seem to be reasonably happy to talk deco-
rously but more or less straightforwardly about it. When it
comes to any behavior not usually on the straight line between
kissing and intercourse, most people are somewhat reticent
unless moved to do a little anonymous verbal exhibitionism
by writing to a sex magazine.

In the past, the medical profession exhibited a moralistic
and judgmental approach to sexual variations. Take, for example, the following quotations from these eminent psychiatrists:

Case 91: Mr. X, civil servant; mother neuropathic, father dia-
betic. . . . Mr. X was of a nervous disposition, but never suffered
from nervous disease, showed no sign of degeneration. . . . At the
age of eight he began spontaneously to masturbate, thinking all
the time of the naked feet of women. . . . At the age of twenty-four,
a great change came over his sexual feelings and his physical condition. He became neurasthenic and began to experience sexual
inclination to males. No doubt excessive masturbation brought

about neurosis and inverted sexuality, to which he was led by excessive desire, remaining unsated by coitus, and by the sight of female feet.... The craving to have sexual intercourse with men grew daily stronger. When he was transferred to a large city, he found the long-wished-for opportunity and actually reveled with intense passion in this unnatural love.

Case 146: One summer's evening, at twilight, X, a doctor of medicine in a North German city, was trodden on by a watchman as he (the doctor) was committing an immoral act.... X comes of a diseased family. His paternal grandfather died by suicide while insane. His father was a weak, peculiar man. One of the patient's brothers masturbated at the age of two. A cousin was sexually perverted and practiced the same immoral acts as X when only a boy, became mentally unstable and died of a spinal disease. A paternal great uncle was a hermaphrodite. His mother's sister was insane. His mother is said to be healthy, but his brother is given to sudden and violent anger.

(R. Krafft Ebing, *Psychopathia Sexualis*, 1886)

The symbolic sadism of women constitutes one of the most remarkable aspects of sexual pathology. No other perversion is so firmly rooted in the individual's general character or pervades all the ordinary activities in like measure as the mental sadism of women. Feminine sadism is invariably totalitarian. We have seen that in many cases perversion in men and women affects character to an inconsiderable extent or not at all and is, in fact, a comparatively isolated phenomenon. But the woman sadist is a sadist through and through and her sadism is the dominant factor in her professional as well as in her social and sexual life.

(M. Hirschfield, *Sexual Anomalies and Perversions*, 1925)

We should make it clear that today this sort of overheated description is very rare. Old attitudes die hard, however, and prejudice flourishes best where there is ignorance. In order, therefore, to avoid value judgments from whatever source, we must start with general descriptions of the range of activities which each type of variant enjoys. This may be going over old ground to readers of some "men's magazines," but we have found that this old ground is in fact sparsely cultivated: nearly all adults, for example, know the sado-sexual image of a woman in an almost stereotypical state of partial undress holding a whip and looking suitably imperious, but many are uncertain as to what really happens in an encounter with such a lady. "Does she actually *use* that thing?" is the most common serious query, for few can believe that it may be possible to do so without causing quite serious damage. But there are many other questions. Let us begin, then with a general description of the range of activities commonly associated with each of our variant groups. This is an impressionistic treatment based on previous research as well as our own. More detailed empirical analysis follows in the next chapter.

FETISHISM

While all of us are more or less aroused by certain aspects of our partners, preferring women with long hair or men with small, neat bottoms, this preference cannot be called fetishism. Traditionally, fetishism occurs when the sexual *goal* is a body part, a fabric or an inanimate object rather than the whole human being. The man who says cheerfully, "I'm a leg man, myself," is not likely to be a fetishist unless he prefers to climax on his partner's legs rather than between them. His attention might be initiated by a woman's legs, but it does not remain there; if further interaction ensues, his aim moves toward the traditional target, preferably in an atmosphere of love and mutual trust, and remains on that target. The fetishist, on the other hand, has his attention focused on the fetish object, and his attention remains almost totally there. He may shift that attention temporarily so that enjoyment of other sex activities can be maximized, but his overall mental orientation will remain inexorably on the fetish object itself. In certain cases, indeed, he will be unable to enjoy sexual satisfaction unless that fetish object is physically present, but this latter contingency should not be used as a criterion of fetishism. A better criterion is whether the man's favorite fantasy is fetish-oriented, regardless of whether the object is physically present. Of course, people may dissemble when questioned on the subject, so in our studies we have used the alternative and

perhaps arbitrary criterion that the fetishist has not only declared himself as finding special erotic pleasure in the fetish
object, whatever it may be, but has joined a club of people
possessing a similar interest. The resultant group scores a significantly higher rating with regard to their interest in fetish
objects than a matched group of people who are not members
of such a group.

One of the curiosities about fetishistic activity these days is
that the focus of attention appears to have changed. Classical
case histories elicit a wide variety of "target" stimuli: parts of
the body (hand, breast, foot, buttock, armpit, hair), body prod-
ucts (sweat, urine, blood), items of clothing (shoes and boots,
handkerchiefs, stockings, underwear, corsets and the more
general category of "uniforms"), materials (satin, velvet,
leather, silk, plastic, rubber) and other inanimate objects such
as baby carriages, cigarette holders and pipes, even collar
studs, safety pins, pieces of crystal and roses. Nowadays, however, fetishism directed toward parts of the body or to objects
which are not items of clothing seems to have become limited
to rare clinical presentations, while a focus on sexy underwear
and a specialized range of garments in rubber, vinyl and
leather appears to have occurred. If this apparent change is
real, it is hardly surprising: society's acceptance of the fact
that "bodies are for touching" has probably reduced the attraction of parts of the body as fetish objects, and the ease of
portraying garments and materials as natural accompaniments
to erotic display has in all likelihood made that type of fetishism more popular and overt. The other fetish objects mentioned above are of interest primarily because of their
uniqueness.

Our descriptions, then, will focus on the garment or material
fetishists that we have studied. Their activities move in one of
two directions, depending on whether the fetishist's partner,
if any, goes along with his predilections to some extent. These
days, a number of them do, and the predilection need not
remain so ghastly a secret as it used to.

If the partner is tolerant, she will dress, or allow him to

dress, in the materials or clothes he finds attractive. This can be a public display if the result does not look ludicrous, but more generally it will be in the privacy of their own home. Sometimes this level of dressing will be the only physical manifestation necessary to make the fetishist happy, as the following quotations from the wives of fetishists show.

"When my husband first told me about his preference, I must admit that I was puzzled, slightly frightened and somewhat resentful. In the end, however, it turned out to be making a bit of a mountain out of a molehill about it. Nowadays I occasionally wear the sort of things he likes me to wear, and, although I think it makes me look a bit stark, it makes him so happy that I haven't the heart to stop it altogether. I mean, it's not as if it was grotesque."

"John builds up tension from his work a bit, and sometimes the strain shows. But if I go upstairs and slip into one of the special dresses he bought me, the tension just flows out of him like melted butter." [John confirmed this, adding that to him the material was "partly arousing, partly relaxing—though I don't suppose you'd understand that."]

"Oh, but we don't take it seriously—it's just a little fun game between us, me dressing up like Snow White's wicked queen before I tell him to take his clothes off, you know." [This example was a little more complex, for in fact the man in question seemed more locked into this ritual than he would admit to his wife. On the other hand, he did not feel it fair to press her into acting out his fantasies more intensely or more frequently than she did already, for as he remarked with some fairness, "I would find it difficult to be as conventional as she would like, so I could hardly expect her to be as unconventional as I would like."]

If the fetishist's behavior is more compulsive, it is less likely that his partner will be as involved, though there are many exceptions to this generalization. The reason for this is simple: as the intensity of fetishistic behavior increases, it becomes clearer that the fetish object, rather than the partner, is the sexual goal. The only hope under such circumstances is that the partner will agree to capitalize on the arousal value of the fetish object, and not every woman will accept such an idea. Some do, however, and many fetishists have paid eloquent tribute to the intense pleasure that they have experienced when partner and fetish are combined during lovemaking.

The more intensive fetishist will generally show a far greater association with the preferred object or material. The underwear fetishist will make collections of undergarments, either the real thing or in photographic form. The fabric fetishist will dress at intervals as completely as possible in his favorite material, often multi-layered, seeking a state where no part of him is left uncovered by the material that turns him on. He will, at this point, almost certainly be alone in his excitation, since his dress usually looks absurd or effeminate and is therefore seldom attractive to a female partner.

It may be observed that the above-mentioned total cover of the body by the fetishist merges into a form of restriction that is in many ways equivalent to the sexual bondage enjoyed by the masochist. At the same time, the reader will doubtless have realized that if a man wishes to wear items which are female in design or material, a link with transvestism is not impossible, though the true fetishist often disclaims the transvestite inference, pointing out that a similar garment made in a material other than his fetishistic preference would have no interest for him. Whether in fact this is so will be discussed later.

We are now some way along the spectrum of fetishistic intensity, and approaching the more extreme modes of behavior. Such extreme behavior is more frequently practiced by someone who lives alone and can indulge his predilection in private as much as he pleases. Those who have a partner are often found to be variant to a more modest degree. The following case history gives an example of the more intense type of fetishist.

Mr. W. is now forty-five years old. He was born of reasonably well-to-do parents, but his father died when Mr. W. was three years old and his mother went to live with her brother at a seaside resort. Mr. W. was an only child, having few friends in his early years, though he does not remember feeling lonely as a result. He got on well with his mother and uncle, did well at school and in

some respects was a "model child." He became passionately interested in natural history, an interest that has persisted all his life,
and states that his first memory of rubber, the fetish material that
now dominates his sexual life, was the smell and feel of a hooded
jacket and overalls made of rubber-backed cotton that he wore
during some of his walks in the country in search of wildlife. "In
such a situation," he says, "one is alone, undistracted by any stimulus coming in and highly sensitized to everything. Under these
circumstances it seems to me inevitable that I should have begun
to turn on to something, especially something which proclaimed
itself, by smell and noise and the heating effect upon my body,
like that rubber did. The odd point about it is that I don't remember it at the time having anything to do with sex."

It was in fact not until the age of fourteen that Mr. W. had what
he describes as "the sort of experience that you psychologist fel-
lows dream about." He had, he says, returned from a country walk,
dressed in his waterproof outfit. He called out to see if his mother
was at home. At first, she didn't answer him, but after a while she
came downstairs and greeted him. After a while, his uncle appeared as well: "And although nothing was said, I somehow was
convinced that they had been having sex together."

Mr. W. has difficulty in remembering how and when he learned
about sex, but feels that he was "reasonably comfortable" as far as
his relationships with girls were concerned. His marriage was
"happy enough" in his own estimation. Never once did he mention his fetishistic leanings to his wife, although he bought appropriate literature and was acquiring a small collection of rubber
garments kept either in the garden shed or in the trunk of his car.
He would dress in these when his wife was out of the house,
achieving orgasm after some time by masturbation. He states that
he was perfectly well able to satisfy his wife sexually by conventional techniques—"and she was the sort of woman that would
have told me if I hadn't satisifed her," he added amicably. His
fantasies during intercourse were, however, nearly always fetish-
oriented.

After fifteen years of marriage, Mr. W.'s wife died. He made no
serious attempt to acquire another partner, because he was "pretty
much able to look after himself" and the appearance of his house
bore this out. His fetish collection grew speedily after his wife's
death, and until recently—for he is at present working on a job
overseas—he kept in his house a complete "rubber room" lined
throughout with curtains of the same material and containing two
large cupboards full of rubber garments, gas masks, photographic
and other equipment. He has in the past visited specialist prosti-

tutes to play out some aspect of his fantasies, but now does not do so, feeling that he has all he needs for sexual satisfaction without leaving his house.

As we said earlier, Mr. W. is an example of an intense fetishist, and it is perhaps advisable to remind the reader that such intensity is uncommon. A more typical case of the same type of fetishism is afforded by Mr. A., whose history is of special interest because he has acquired a female partner who in adult life has begun to share Mr. A.'s predilection.

Mr. A. is fifty-two years old and comes from a working-class family. He did not have a close relationship with his father as a child, though it improved later. His relationship with his mother was unremarkable. Mr. A.'s grandparents, who lived nearby, were looked after by an aunt whom everybody loved and who became a central figure in Mr. A.'s life. Grandfather was "a martinet"—a strict disciplinarian. The aunt was totally dependent on him and brought up as "God-fearing and in an atmosphere of spiritualism." Mr. A. has an early memory of her dressed in a leather coat which he has described in detail: he developed fantasies involving her dressed in this coat, which he remembers incorporating into masturbation rituals in the privacy of his bedroom at about the age of seven.

Three years later he developed an interest in his brother's rubberized raincoat, wearing it "while playing with the tap in the kitchen," but was chastised for getting wet and did not do so again. He then became attached to his own school mackintosh, remembering clearly the smell and feel of it and that he enjoyed playing, while dressed in this raincoat and rubber boots, in a flooded brook near his home.

At this stage, his aunt would always meet him from school when it was raining, wearing a rubberized mackintosh herself and, if necessary, bringing him his own raincoat. In many instances she encouraged him to wear the garment. He claims, indeed, that "she was hooked on rubber in whatever form that came to hand." During puberty, the two of them always chose her new mackintosh together in a specific store every autumn. According to Mr. A., the choice was unhurried, with much trying on of different models. He also describes in detail a certain afternoon's shelter beneath a tree in the rain, both of them dressed appropriately, when the conversation moved guardedly but unmistakably to the sexuality implicit in wearing rubber, and his aunt's not unpleased reaction to the event. After what, to Mr. A. at least, was an idyllic relationship, it is sad to have to record that the lady in question became mentally unstable and was later placed in an asylum.

Mr. A. now has his own business. His wife knows of his predilection for rubber and has on various occasions cooperated with his wishes for her to wear it while having sex. She is, however, uninterested in it herself. Because of ill health on her part and possibly because of his current relationship with Miss Y., of whom we shall speak in a moment, Mr. A. has not forced the issue at all. In fact, he claims that he has no wish to do so. He reasons that his wife must know that Miss Y. is catering to his liking by wearing a rubber mackintosh at intervals when their work together demands, for instance when it is raining and they are working outside. However, none of the three persons involved mention the fact openly to one another.

Mr. A.'s fetishistic pattern is similar to that of Miss Y. Neither goes in for occlusion (the total cover-up with breathing and movement restricted—which is very popular in fetishistic pornography) or restriction of any kind, nor do they have any desire to occlude or restrict their partner. Both stress the extra sexual excitement that heavy rain gives them when they are appropriately dressed, an excitement also created by artificial rain in the form of a hose-pipe spray. Both have solo sessions as well as sessions together.

We have at Mr. A.'s request refrained from contacting Mrs. A. directly, but we gain the impression from both Mr. A. and Miss Y. that the marriage, of many years standing, is stable and very happy, with shared interests in music and, as Mr. A. put it quite simply, each other.

Miss Y. is forty-two years old, born of a working-class family with high social ambitions. Education at primary and secondary schools appears to have been uneventful. As a child she was, in her own words, "shy but tomboyish." She became the Akela of the local Wolf Cub pack. She started work at sixteen, and progressed well, having a natural flair for figures. Noting the limited mental and career horizons of her female companions and the fact that they often "had to get married," she resolved to be different in both respects. At twenty-three, however, she suffered a minor nervous breakdown due to overwork and an excessive sense of responsibility toward her Cub pack. She moved elsewhere and, in the course of her new job (during which her shyness largely disappeared), met Mr. and Mrs. A. Three years later, during which time her friendship with both developed but no sexual relationship with Mr. A. appeared, she was invited by Mr. A. to work for him in his business. She was not aware of Mr. A.'s liking for rubber at this stage, and both she and he state that they have no memory of the offer having been made for anything more than business reasons. Soon after accepting Mr. A.'s offer, however, she noticed, since work took them out together a lot, the effect of rubber clothing on Mr. A. She tried the effect of this material by placing it in direct contact with her body, and immediately and somewhat unnervingly found it sexually arousing. She repeated the process on subsequent occasions, orgasm frequently occurring as a result. She confided her actions to Mr. A. and other garments were bought. Considerable closeness developed between them, but the relationship with Mrs. A. was not impaired. They have had several "sessions" together—no intercourse, but mutual petting while both wear, and thus are separated by, rubber clothing. The onset of rain quickly arouses them, as does the smell of warm rubber. Living alone, Miss Y. is able to have solo sessions of dressing in the material, achieving multiple (six or seven) orgasms as a result. Attempts to prolong and intensify the sessions further have been tried but have not been found advantageous. She finds no pleasure in occlusion or restriction, and states that she is not masochistic. She has had other successful sexual relationships, none allied with rubber, but remains unmarried.

It is worth recording that both in correspondence and in conversation with Miss Y., we have gained the impression that she is content with her situation, and is concerned that her relationship with Mr. A. shall not mar the friendship that she has with Mrs. A. nor the very happy marriage that, according to her, Mr. and Mrs. A. have.

These are of course only two examples of fetishistic behavior. Many other variations are possible and are in fact found. While we have chosen them to be representative of two intensity levels in the area, it is inevitable that any case study will be atypical in certain respects, no matter how much it corresponds to the average or "stereotypic" pattern. Thus female fetishism in its intrinsically motivated form, as opposed to that which is simply engaged in to please a male partner, is quite rare, so Mr. A. can count himself lucky to have secured the companionship of Miss Y. It is equally unusual for the development of a fetishistic interest to be encouraged by a female adult in the manner of Mr. A.'s aunt, although we do not know the extent to which this was merely the way Mr. A. perceived her attitude. It is all these exceptions that limit the usefulness of the case-history approach to behavioral analysis, and the reason that quantitative techniques like those to be described in the next chapter are necessary to provide supplementary information. Equally, the collective and average results can often obscure the rich complexities of individual cases.

SADOMASOCHISM

The behavior pattern of sadomasochism is more complex, involving any one or more of a number of activities. These include direct beating with the hand or with a wide variety of instruments (paddle, belt, cane and whip being the most popular); pricking, cutting and burning; tying up, gagging, blindfolding and immobilization in stocks and pillories; besides the more general category of forcing someone to do something which they do not wish to do. Allied to these physical activities is the mental technique of humiliation, which may be either purely verbal, pouring scorn or abuse upon the victim, or situational, in which the victim is dressed in a belittling costume before performing demeaning tasks.

It is our impression, however, based on our interviews and the research of others, that in reality, most sexual sadists have no wish to hurt their partner in their sex games any more than is enjoyed or at least accepted by that partner. A masochist has little wish to put his head on the block, figuratively or literally, and will only play that role with someone who understands the "rules of the game." Let us not at this stage get into involved theories of why this hypothesis might be true, and we will also for the moment disregard certain classical case histories in which appalling cruelties are linked with sexually oriented behavior. Instead, let us listen to sadomasochists in interviews.

> "My wife and I do play dominance and submission games, and maybe we have the marks to prove it on occasion. But the one playing top dog watches like a hawk to make sure we stop when the other one doesn't like it any more."

"Of course, he doesn't *really* hurt me. I mean quite recently he tied me down ready to receive 'punishment,' then by mistake he kicked my heel with his toe as he walked by. I gave a yelp, and he said, 'Sorry love—did I hurt you?' "

[After examining a sadomasochistic drawing:] "Terrific! Not that I'd dream of really doing anything like that."

These statements are typical of the subjects that we have investigated, though we admit that they need not be true of other, less approachable people of the same genre. The quarterly magazine published by the society for sadomasochists, from whose members much of our data was gleaned, nevertheless reflects the self-mocking appreciation of the fact that a lot of what goes on is in the mind. As a lady with such tendencies once put it to us with a smile, "I would like to be savagely beaten and brutally treated by a man who wouldn't ever dream of hurting me at all."

Two cartoons from the society's magazines further illustrate this. The first depicts a woman strapped to a diabolically complex piece of equipment smiling happily up at a man who is saying angrily, "What do you mean, 'Have you put the cat out?' " In the other, two prisoners are seen chained to a wall, one far more stressfully than the other. The less-chained one views the retreating form of a clearly female torturer and says mournfully, "I wish she liked me like she does you."

If, then, we are to claim that sadomasochists are not as a rule truly dangerous, what are we to make of the Jack the Rippers of this world? Here we merely suggest that additional factors contribute to produce the uncaring, psychopathic qualities associated with the sexually dangerous individual. As long as a reasonable number of people exist who call themselves sadomasochistic and play games of that kind, yet who are accepted by their partners or others as not being dangerous, we have to admit that sadomasochism *per se* is not as dreadful as uninformed society might believe.

To illustrate the point, let us take a double case history where the "violence" is up to a point real, but seems adequately controlled within the ritual of sex.

Mr. B. is now twenty-eight years old. His birth was induced two months prematurely because of his mother's ill health, which in general was not good: her record notes two nervous breakdowns. His father was in the army, and was frequently away from home during the first five years of his son's life. Mr. B.'s childhood relationships with his parents were not good. He reports considerable anxiety and tension, that he was a battered baby, and that he experienced jealousy of his older sister. His development was retarded: he did not walk until he was four years old, and spoke very little until five years of age. He had coordination difficulties between eye and hand, had severe speech difficulties around the ages of six and seven and stammered considerably. He was—and still is, to a lesser extent—dyslexic. He had night terrors, images of eyes, especially eyes in sculptures. He walked in his sleep, had occasional bedwetting episodes and was quite dependent on his pacifier.

During this period, his mother held deep religious convictions, believing firmly that she had visits from the saints, "saw" St. Christopher several times and "spoke with God." Mr. B. was thus brought up in a highly religious atmosphere but "broke with religion at twelve years old after a furious argument with a priest, as a result of which I was excommunicated." The relationship between his parents was not good: "Father was impotent, at least with mother, and they haven't had sex for many years." At this point he was asked how he knew these details so well and, surprisingly, replied, "My mother adores me and confides everything to me."

His early school experiences were uneventful but probably partly ineffectual because of his dyslexia and difficulty in socializing. As he puts it, "I had virtually no friends until I was about ten years old." However, on transferring to a small boarding school with little competitive spirit, he began to make good progress, both in work and play, and became a good cricketer. He is now verbally fluent, perfectly sociable and, although often lamenting his ignorance of a number of subjects, shows no evidence of his early retardation.

His relationships with his teachers at school were divided. He hated his female teachers and idolized his male teachers. His first awareness of sex began at fourteen years, when he discovered masturbation. He claims that he felt neither prudish nor guilty about this practice, and had no early homosexual feelings. "In fact," he says, "I tried homosexuality later. It didn't work; I didn't like it." He first experienced intercourse at about eighteen years old with a woman of forty-five who, he says, seduced him. "At the time," he adds as if by way of explanation, "I was very much a male chauvinist, did the motorcycle bit, but it passed. I was frightened of smashing my face up—I'm terrified of operations anyway, afraid of losing control of myself, losing my identity under an anaesthetic."

On meeting his wife-to-be, he was attracted by the contrast between the two of them. "She was warm, weak and willing, and I could easily dominate her," he said. Perhaps it should be noted that this statement was made with neither hostility nor coldness. His wife was in the room when he made the statement and he smiled happily at her. She in turn took no exception to his words, but giggled delightedly. After one month they were living together, and after one year they were married.

Mr. B. had found his first masochistic girlfriend at twenty, "training" her according to his sexual pattern—as he did his wife, later. His work pattern at that stage was not stable, "though this was largely because of my absence of paper qualifications and my dyslexia, which meant that my writing skill was primitive. But my work in the stage and stage-props world brought me into many experiences—some good, some bad. I met many unusual people. I got an ulcer, though I seldom drink. I have taken drugs, though I've given them up now. I had one emotional collapse from the drug scene, and that scared me. I lost control, so I stopped."

"At first," he continues, discussing his married life, "I was convinced that I could not love, and in spite of our domination activities, our general sex life was not good. Now it is good—very good. My wife has convinced me that I am capable of being loved. True, we do play sex games a lot. One day my wife went down to the pub dressed like a tart, and I went down later and picked her up like a john. It was fantastic."

Mr. and Mrs. B.'s sadomasochistic activities are intense, with dramatic overtones. Mr. B. likes to enclose his wife entirely in some sort of sack, using bondage, gagging and semi-suffocation. He will throw her violently onto the bed, tie her up and use a cane or even a whip on her: "I have to make her cry so that she can obtain an orgasm." His wife actively welcomes what he does to her: his "brutality," real and symbolic, is not only pleasurable to him but is a welcome trigger for her sexual release. It is thus necessary to read Mrs. B.'s case history in order to set their relationship in perspective. At the time the double case-history report was taken, Mr. and Mrs. B. were happy and relaxed. They have two attractive children and no more problems and idiosyncrasies than the average family. Mr. B. has a steady job, while his wife is happy in her role of housewife and mother.

Mrs. B. is now thirty-one years old. Her birth was normal, and her parents' health good. She was brought up by both parents, who are both living. Although she prefers her mother, her relationships with both parents are good. She has one older sister and two younger ones. She does not get along too well with her older sister, stating that her sister, who suffered during her formative years from the deprivations of the war when their father was away much of the time, is therefore jealous of her.

Mrs. B.'s school years and childhood development were normal and apparently uneventful. She did quite well at school where she classed herself as a tomboy. Her boyish figure and short hair still give that impression, although her attitudes and statements belie this. She learned about sex from her mother: her reaction to the education was positive, filling her with a "sense of thrill and wonder." She nevertheless remembers feeling a degree of prudishness about the matter for some years, "perhaps because I was brought up in a convent school, where the attitudes conflicted with my own," she adds. She has no lesbian tendencies, though she admires what she calls "their freedom." "Lesbian films have a sort of beauty about them," she says, as if still thinking it out.

Her father's attitude toward feminine sexuality was quite specific, and Mrs. B. is convinced that this attitude deeply affected her own development. "He was very dominant, but protective," she says. "He was in love with a film star while we were growing up, and he believed that we should be like her—even look like her and dress like her. He had this image of woman as a dumb little sexpot, and told us that we should be like her and be glamorous and sexy twenty-four hours a day. And no way could I do this, so I ended up with a sort of emotional frigidity due to lack of sexual confidence."

Mrs. B. had a very fantasy-filled puberty, developing images of being raped by a cowboy "so that I could claim that it wasn't my fault," she adds. "The wilder the fantasies were, the more I wondered if I was crazy. My father was terrified of insanity: he thought that if you walked with your feet turned out or your eyebrows met in the middle, you were crazy. As for doing anything kinky . . ."

According to Mrs. B., the strain of trying to live up to the impossible socio-sexual target that her father set her began to tell. She became a near-alcoholic—or, at least, she was dependent on alcohol—before she met Mr. B. She now drinks far less, though she likes a drink, claiming that it makes her more sexually aroused and releases her inhibitions.

Her first real experience of sex was with Mr. B., and she did not object to his introducing her to sadomasochism as a sexual accompaniment. "In fact," she said, "although he introduced me to it gradually, I found the masks he wanted me to wear welcome, because I could relax and be myself behind them, unseen. I also like wearing heavy makeup, possibly for the same reason. It must be a question of release: when my husband beats me—sexually, that is—and makes me cry, all my sexuality floods out of me, and it is wonderful."

The form of Mr. and Mrs. B.'s lovemaking has been described above, but has many other elements of ritual. In their play-games, she must change costume every hour, on the hour, or according to his whims, and is "punished" for inattention to detail, lateness or forgetfulness. She enjoys lovemaking while wanting to urinate—"He doesn't let me go to the toilet without permission"—and is sometimes shocked by her own desires, although she enjoys the shock. One of the most interesting facets of the relationship between them is that his cruelty toward her is entirely confined to the sexual aspect. His kindness and attentiveness toward her and the deep affection between them was apparent throughout the interviews.

Although the sadistic behavior shown by Mr. B. is real, it seems moderate in its intensity. Examination of other cases, however, has convinced us that the masochist will accept and enjoy quite extreme treatment, readily returning for more on subsequent occasions. In our researches, we initially made the mistake of believing too readily what our subjects told us. Finding, however, that some of the tales we were told as fact turned out to be pure fantasy, we thereafter checked more carefully. Then it was our turn to be surprised: body marks from cane or whip were not uncommon, while reports of burning with hot wax, cigarette burns, tattooing, nose- or nipple-piercing and other activities are rarer but not always mere fantasy.

A number of theories have been put forward to account for why the masochist should value the pain that turns him on, but very few explanations have been advanced as to how such intensely painful stimuli seem to be transmuted into pleasure by certain people. As an elderly neurologist (himself a masochist) has put it to us:

When a person such as myself visits a sympathetic lady so that he might obtain pleasure by her inflicting what most people regard as pain on him, a curious thing happens. With me at any rate, the stimulus must be applied at a very modest intensity at first. As my ritual is carried out, the intensity may be increased without my finding it distressing. By the time climax occurs, the woman is beating me with an intensity that, were it done outside the situation we have arranged, would probably give me a heart attack, while my cries would be heard far away. It is by no means easy to explain how such high levels of pain can be not only tolerated but enjoyed.

It is no doubt this paradox which alienates society, making it difficult to accept sadomasochism as just one of those things that people enjoy. It seems hard to believe that the sadist might be completely harmless and that the "victim" might be enjoying the whole business immensely.

TRANSVESTISM

Like sadomasochism, transvestism is a complex phenomenon about which there are a number of misconceptions. It is characterized *only* by a wish to dress in the clothes of the opposite sex: it has no particular association with homosexuality; it does not necessarily imply effeminacy, nor a lasting wish to belong to the opposite sex. Because there is no wish to change sex physically, it can be distinguished from transsexualism. The wish to cross-dress can of course be expressed in theory by both sexes: in practice, most transvestites are men who like to dress in female clothes.

Even the simplest questioning of those who do wish to cross-dress, however, reveals that there are several types of transvestite, differentiated by their attitudes towards the activity. The various types have perhaps best been characterized by Harry Benjamin in his book, *The Transsexual Phenomenon.* The four relevant distinctions are as follows.

The pseudotransvestite is not a true transvestite at all. He tries cross-dressing as an exploratory behavior. He has perhaps realized that a woman with a minimum of very feminine clothing on seems visually more attractive to him than does a totally naked one, and decides to find out whether any of that appeal resides in the clothes themselves. He tries them on and either decides that they do very little for him or that, because of the novelty of the activity, they are arousing but perhaps not as much in the long run as the woman who wears them. Alternatively, he may have a very lively curiosity about what it feels like, in a purely tactile sense, to be a woman. He notices that (until recently, at least) a fairly high proportion of women's clothes, such as girdles, garter belts, high-heeled shoes and tight dresses, seem in theory uncomfortable to wear. Believing, therefore, that there might be advantages to be gained from the discomfort of such attire, he tries them both to judge that discomfort and to discover any compensation that might ensue. In all cases, the episodes are carried out largely for kicks rather than because of any real need or desire. In any case, the pseudotransvestite feels masculine, has a largely conventional male sex life, may indulge in transvestite fantasies occasionally but never considers any further action in that direction.

The fetishistic transvestite dresses periodically in female clothes, but his reason for doing so is that the clothes act as fetish objects and give him a great deal of sexual arousal—sometimes as much as, or even more than, contact with a real live woman. For such men there is very little wish to be wholly a woman, only a fairly intense desire to act as one in certain quite limited and rather stereotyped ways. These ways are not womanly as a whole, but mimic a particular type of woman by expressing a desire to show off, to be adored or adulated, to be over-theatrical and artificially sexy—in short, to be taken notice of. A strong clue to the fact that real womanhood is not desired is our observation that this group contains a high proportion of masochistic men with the desire to be "humiliated" by being made to dress as a woman, and others who opt for a fairly exotic costume with long wig, jewelry, false eyelashes, earrings and the like. Neither of these images is typical of womanhood as a whole. Since the orien-

tation is fetishistic rather than identificatory, this type of transvestite still feels masculine, lives as a man, is generally
heterosexual and rejects any idea of changing sex. He may
have guilt feelings about his predilection, and if this builds up
excessively, therapy may be useful. Generally, however, this
type can live with his state without trouble.

The "true" transvestite still classes himself as masculine,
but seems less convinced about the matter. He cross-dresses
frequently, practicing female ways and taking advice from the
growing number of shops selling makeup and women's clothing which, often quietly, have someone sympathetic around
to advise the transvestite. This type may indeed now live and
be accepted as a woman, or at least wear female clothing
under his male dress if he has no other chance. Cross-dressing
is not intended to arouse sexually, but to relax. The major kind
of satisfaction obtained is not so much sexual as one of relief
from gender discomfort. In spite of this, he is still basically
heterosexual in orientation, even if preferring a supine position during lovemaking. When cross-dressed, however, his
orientation is more often toward a male partner, but since the
transvestite in this state no longer considers himself a man but
totally a woman, the question of whether the relationship (fantasy or fact) is homosexual or not becomes a matter of definition.

It is at this point that the transvestite becomes in some ways
most interesting. He is "betwixt and between." He actually
rejects a real sex-change operation, though the idea is attractive to him; he is, therefore, still not transsexual, even in in-
tent. He will experiment with estrogen if he can obtain it, for
this is a female hormone which will assist the development of
breast tissue and reduce the male libido. Both of these
changes can be useful to him, for he can gain some insight as
to whether his liking for cross-dressing is for arousal purposes
or for relief from gender discomfort. He may, if puzzled about
his apparently intersexual status, go for some form of psychotherapy, but this is likely to be less successful for the true
transvestite than for the fetishistic cross-dresser.

Another means of coping with his situation is to assume a form of dual personality, one male, one female, with a different name attached to each. The two personalities are actually measurably different: research has shown (Gosselin and Eysenck, 1980) that if "true" transvestites fill in the *Eysenck Personality Questionnaire* while in their male role and then repeat the process while cross-dressed and functioning as a female, the results show more extraversion and significantly less neuroticism as they change from male to female. This ties in with the statement made by this type of transvestite that they feel more relaxed when cross-dressed, or that indeed they feel "a different person" under these circumstances. However schizophrenic and self-deluding this might appear to the outsider, it quite often appears to be a successful way of coming to terms with the problem.

The transsexual. While we have only limited information on those labelling themselves "transsexuals," it is as well to quote Benjamin's criteria for distinguishing the transsexual states from those that we have already considered. Benjamin distinguishes three transsexual types, the first being nonsurgical but involving the use of feminizing estrogen. The sex drive is constantly low, but cross-dressing is fairly compulsive. Psychotherapy is either refused or is unsuccessful, because the preferred gender-orientation is still somewhat undecided. Benjamin's last two classifications differ from each other largely in intensity of femininity, but both involve a definite female gender-orientation and a strong need to live and work as a woman. The sex-change operation is striven for, and frequently obtained—indeed, there seems in the high-intensity transsexual such a complete hatred of his male sex organs that the danger of suicide or self-mutilation must always be recognized if the sex-change operation is "illogically" delayed. As a result, much research has gone into distinguishing between the transsexual and the transvestite, in order that any sex-change operation shall neither be denied to those who really would be better off as a member of the opposite sex, nor given to someone who might later regret it. Both denial and premature conversion have unfortunately been reported in the past, and mistakes can be tragic either way. Neil Buhrich and Neil McConaghy, both working in Sydney, Australia, have probably done most to set out the differences: in 1977 they published a study in which they classified the transsexual as generally young, single, cross-dressed fully, reporting past homosexual experience, a feminine gender-identity (even to the extent of always sitting to urinate) and stating a desire for sex-change surgery. In comparison, the transvestites reported significantly more heterosexual interest, cross-dressed partially, were older, generally married and reported that the female clothes that they wore aroused them sexually. Other workers have reported other differences, and although some clinicians have warned of the ease with which some transvestites can be misclassified as transsexuals (and vice versa), there seems little doubt that transvestism and transsexualism are different entities and not merely different intensities of the same desire to experience femaleness.

Our studies, however, have been mostly with transvestites rather than transsexuals, and it is to them we shall return. By way of introduction to what we would term a "typical" (true) transvestite case history, let us quote from his introductory letter to us: we can confirm that, whether as John or as Jenny, he has a helpful, clear picture of his situation.

Over the years I have achieved the ability to pass as a woman, unlikely as this would seem if you met me as John. My friends think that the metamorphosis is remarkable, and many comment that even my personality changes dramatically. My female life is a complete holiday from my normal self, and many of the answers that I have given in your questionnaire would be quite different if I answered as Jenny. I have a circle of friends as Jenny, some of whom do not know that I am a man. I go on holiday with a couple who are older than I and are taken by some to be my parents. As Jenny I hold parties at which I can very much keep the party going, though John in the same circumstances would find this heavy going.

My father was a brilliant man, but was an alcoholic and frequently away on business. As a result, my principal dilemma was that, having grown up with a very good mother and two sisters, I instinctively knew the woman's role but not the man's. As a man I have consciously to ask myself how I should behave, and as such I fall back on a formal, polite, innocuous sort of nothingness. As Jenny, I am positive, vital and at ease, usually the life and soul of the party and certainly more light-hearted. Being Jenny adds a little verve to everything I do, and I enjoy helping newcomers to the transvestite scene to get rid of their guilt and to get the thing in perspective, so that transvestism is an added bonus rather than a problem for them.

There is much self-deception to transvestism, as you must know. I have tried to face it squarely and simply to enjoy this rather stupid perversion. I think I have learned to contain it, and find that it is a tiger that I can ride with some exhilaration, but in no sense is it now my master. I am unconcerned by several months of enforced restraint—if my mother comes to stay with me, for example —but when I do indulge, I like to do it properly for a week or so. I can't stand the privileged gatherings where bizarre amateurs sit around in high heels and fishnet tights inviting compliments on their stage makeup. They seem to be emotionally immature and, like psychotics, they inhabit castles in the air—for which, as you must know, the psychiatrist collects the rent. I still build the odd castle, but at least I know why I'm doing it. The pleasure comes mainly from the fact that one can indulge feelings which are generally regarded as foreign to a man. I like the realistic straightforwardness of women to the everyday affairs of life—the lack of stuffiness, the light-hearted disregard for men's conventions, the freedom from men's uniform mode of dress. It's nice to be able to ask for help, which John never does, and it's lovely to get a warm response and to feel that mysterious alchemy that enlivens any encounter with a man.

I have no conscious homosexual tendencies—in fact, I find the idea repulsive—but when I am Jenny I am decidedly polarized by a man that I like. It calls forth a sort of coquettishness which in turn usually evokes an agreeable response, and all this feels entirely natural. I am protected from overfamiliarity by my age and, I am told, by the fact that I behave as a professional sort of woman: I have degrees in both medicine and engineering, though I do not push the fact because it lands me in endless discussions of gall bladders or bridges.

Yet for all my ability to talk about dressmaking and cooking, I know in my heart that I can never be a real woman, so I will never consider the operation. As John, I have too many interesting hobbies that would be difficult to pursue in bra, skirt and wig.

In the above letter one can see quite clearly the extent and the limit of John/Jenny's transvestism. The "dual personality" comes over clearly, and indeed on meeting John one is struck by his retiring, quietly analytical nature—a facet of his character which enables him to observe, with meticulous accuracy, the small differences between masculine and feminine habits and thus to make Jenny "another thing altogether."

Mr. J. is fifty-seven years old, although as Jenny he looks about forty. His birth was normal, his health good and his mother's health and disposition were unexceptional. As has been mentioned before, his father was an alcoholic, possibly (according to Mr. J.) because of *his* father's repressive and over-religious nature. In spite of the alcoholism, however, the relationship between the parents was good, and so was Mr. J.'s relationship with his parents. Friends of the family were very supportive, and the family survived as a unit. There were three younger sisters (three, nine and twelve years younger), with whom Mr. J. got along well. His development was normal, and he was happy enough at school except for minor bullying due to his extreme nearsightedness. It is interesting to note here that, while John wears glasses, Jenny wears contact lenses.

Mr. J. first cross-dressed at the age of eight or nine. Why did he do it? "I think," he says uncertainly, still unsure after many attempts to discover his own motivations, "it was to gain . . . well, not attention, but a sort of favor from my father. I thought he favored the girls in the family . . . they were allowed to do things like show emotions, which as a boy I was not supposed to do—stiff upper lip, and all that. Of course, I didn't display my cross-dressing to my father, though."

Mr. J. learned about sex—more or less correctly, as he remembers—at school. He had no adolescent traumas that he remembers, except the quiet and rather puzzled knowledge that dressing as a girl attracted him. He had no social reticence, plenty of girlfriends, did well in higher education and had a number of good jobs, including his own medical practice. He got married, though the marriage broke down after just over a year on the issue of his transvestism—not his defiant determination to be allowed to be transvestite, but simply his wife's discovery of the fact. There were attempts at reconciliation, but these were unsuccessful. Later there was a second marriage which lasted seven years: Mr. J. told his second wife of his variant predilection before they were wed. This second marriage ended in a sort of drifting apart due to what

Mr. J. classes as "just a lack of sex interest on my part." The couple are now separated and Mr. J. lives alone, switching from John to Jenny as circumstances permit and as he feels inclined.

In an endeavor to touch the wellspring of his attitude towards his transvestite activities, we asked him whether he would feel happier if people were allowed to dress as they wished. From John's rather reserved attitude suddenly sprung something of Jenny's greater mischievousness. "Heavens, no," he smiled. "Merely to be allowed to wear women's clothes in public is nothing. It is the challenge of being so much like a woman that no one knows I'm a man that turns me on. The combination of doing something that I want to, that everyone says is impossible and is forbidden anyway, produces in me an arousal which, because it is in a sexual context, becomes sexual arousal." Quite a theory, although one which he freely admits may not be true for every transvestite.

From the above it can be seen that John/Jenny is a transvestite and not a transsexual. He belongs in the older age group, has had heterosexual experiences, has been married, does not particularly hate his male genitalia and certainly values being a man as well as a woman. He has never expressed any real wish for a sex-change operation, although he clearly enjoys being able to pass as a woman when he wishes, and while it is debatable whether the arousal he experiences from cross-dressing is sexual or not, the reasons he gives for so doing seem to have nothing to do with feeling *more* natural as a woman than as a man.

We do not wish, however, to go too deeply at this stage. This chapter has sought merely to give a flavor of the activities traditionally carried out by the three main groups studied in this book. It is now time to examine the new findings based on our Sex Fantasy Questionnaire.

4

Comparing Sexual Patterns

So far we have confined ourselves to a purely descriptive account of the activities associated with fetishism, sadomasochism and transvestism, and it is time for us to examine what other differences there might be between those who practice such variations and those who do not. In some ways it is curious that we should even wish to do this, for people who are fanatics about many other activities seldom come in for such scrutiny. The man who collects stamps or butterflies with obsessional passion is left to pursue his hobby without society's comment; the man who collects panties is not. The man who spends hours photographing wild birds does so with no more than a flicker of interest from those about him; the man who spends the same time photographing girls who have been bound and gagged generally does so in some secrecy. The man who enjoys fancy dress parties is regarded as a healthy and good-humored extravert, but the man who wears a woman's nightie while making love is regarded with suspicion if not outright hostility.

Both those whose love-lives are conventional and those whose are not are interested in whether or not there are "real" differences between them, apart from their declared sexual preferences. Those with conventional tastes sometimes seem to wish to have proved to them the fact that there are such differences. Those with unconventional tastes generally wish us to help them prove that no "real" differences exist. Even the observation of this partisanship was, to our way of thinking, somewhat sad.

Let us nevertheless turn to our findings from the *Wilson Sexual Fantasy Questionnaire* and establish what differences might exist between the conventional and less conventional sex-patterned groups. If we begin by examining the ten most popular fantasies reported by each group (Table 1) we see that the transvestites show a very similar set of preferred fantasies to that shown by those of conventional sexual tastes—apart, of course, from the former's interest in cross-dressing and the sexual arousal obtained from the clothing and materials involved. The sadomasochists and fetishists, on the other hand, show a rather different pattern from that of the control group, with a variety of special fantasies displacing the more conventional, intimate ones.

More surprising, perhaps, but apparently not in the least unexpected to those involved, is the popularity of fetishistic fantasies among sadomasochists; in fact, it overshadows even their own defining predilections. Also fairly striking is the degree of sadomasochistic fantasy in the fetishistic group. Altogether, there is a great deal of similarity between the sadomasochists and fetishists.

Another way to look at the differences in fantasy and behavior among the various groups is to compare their average ratings for each theme in turn. These are given in Table 2.

Making love out of doors in a romantic setting. All of the groups appear to have a low rating for this fantasy, but in fact this is not exceptional, for people generally have fantasies with many elements and select different elements on different occasions. Three out of four of our variant groups score significantly lower than the control group. Whether this is due to their having a less romantic attitude towards sex or a dislike

Table 1. The ten most popular fantasies (in order of preference) of variant and control groups.

Sado-masochists	Rubberites	Leatherites	Transvestites	Controls
1. Excited by material or clothing	Excited by material or clothing	Excited by material or clothing	Wearing clothes of opposite sex	Intercourse with known partner
2. Being whipped or spanked	Masturbation to orgasm by partner	Being tied up	Excited by materials or clothing	Intercourse with loved partner
3. Being tied up	Being tied up	Being forced to do something	Intercourse with loved partner	Receiving oral sex
4. Intercourse with known partner	Intercourse with loved partner	Giving oral sex	Kissing passionately	Taking someone's clothes off
5. Being forced to do something	Kissing passionately	Masturbation to orgasm by partner	Intercourse with known partner	Giving oral sex
6. Masturbation to orgasm by partner	Intercourse with known partner	Intercourse with loved partner	Receiving oral sex	Kissing passionately
7. Intercourse with loved partner	Receiving oral sex	Intercourse with known partner	Having clothes taken off	Masturbation to orgasm by partner
8. Taking someone's clothes off	Being forced to do something	Receiving oral sex	Being much sought after by opposite sex	Sex elsewhere than in bedroom
9. Kissing passionately	Sex with someone much younger	Tying someone up	Taking someone's clothes off	Sex with someone much younger
10. Being hurt by partner	Giving oral sex	Being whipped or spanked	Giving oral sex	Having clothes taken off

of taking it outdoors remains to be seen. The latter seems likely to have some validity, since many rubberites associate wet weather outdoors with arousal, and this might explain why their score on this item is higher than the leatherite group.

Having intercourse with a loved partner. Here there is no significant difference between the groups—an interesting finding if one had supposed that sexual variation alienates people from loved partners. Sadomasochists and rubberites fantasize slightly more than average on this theme, although the control group reports the highest level of activity.

Having intercourse with someone you know but have not yet had sex with. Although both the fetishistic and the transvestite groups show less inclination to fantasize on this theme than does the control group, only the transvestites have a significantly lower rating. Does this indicate that the transvestite is, perhaps, imitating the stereotypic woman, supposedly shy about starting new sexual relationships?

Having intercourse with an anonymous stranger. This theme shows the same pattern as the previous one, with the transvestite group showing significantly less fantasy and activity on this subject. We shall notice a comparative lack of interest by this group in a number of themes yet to be discussed.

Sex with two other people and *participating in an orgy* are two traditionally "swinging" themes, but no group showed any significant difference from the average. Perhaps surprisingly, the level of the ratings shows that, for all the attention paid in sex magazines to these themes, only rarely do these fantasies occur on average in either the conventionally or the less conventionally sex-patterned male mind. The behaviors themselves are of course rarer still.

Being forced to do something. One would expect the sadomasochistic group rating to be significantly high here, but, surprisingly, all the variant groups fantasize and act significantly more on this theme. The theme of *forcing someone to do something* shows the same high rating among the sadomasochistic group, but the differences are smaller (though still significant) for the fetishists, and disappear altogether for the transvestites. These overall lower ratings may seem strange to the outsider, for the control group ratings are higher for "forcing" than "being forced," and one might expect a natural preference for *not* being the victim.

Homosexual activity. The spread of results on this theme makes the differences between the average ratings difficult to interpret. Homosexual fantasies loom slightly larger in the minds of members of the variant groups than in those of the control group, but the difference is significant only for the sadomasochistic group. Of course, this higher mean score need not be spread evenly over all members of the group; it

Table 2. Mean ratings of variant and control groups for fantasy and activity for each theme in the Sex Fantasy Questionnaire.

As explained on pages 19–20, the scores for this and similar tables are mean ratings based on a numerical scale that represents frequencies of activity (or fantasy) from "never"—0—to "regularly"—5. (Column F is the fantasy rating and column A is activity).

	Sado-masochists		Rubberites		Leatherites		Transvestites		Controls	
	F	A	F	A	F	A	F	A	F	A
1. Making love out of doors in a romantic setting (e.g. field of flowers, beach at night).	0.80	1.00	0.96	1.26	0.34	1.03	0.70	0.91	1.24	1.62
2. Having intercourse with a loved partner.	2.16	3.14	2.13	3.16	1.90	3.34	1.80	3.36	1.95	3.70
3. Intercourse with someone you know but have not had sex with.	2.43	0.79	1.96	0.41	1.91	0.50	1.47	0.33	2.13	0.94
4. Intercourse with an anonymous stranger.	1.44	0.83	1.18	0.40	1.17	0.63	0.86	0.29	1.33	0.94
5. Sex with two other people.	1.59	0.71	1.12	0.36	1.36	0.89	0.85	0.24	1.11	0.56
6. Participating in an orgy.	1.20	0.31	1.00	0.14	1.36	0.39	0.55	0.12	1.10	0.36
7. Being forced to do something.	2.40	1.75	1.81	0.87	2.11	1.29	1.30	0.38	0.19	0.12
8. Forcing someone to do something.	1.53	0.85	1.15	0.69	1.33	1.16	0.35	0.22	0.56	0.40
9. Homosexual activity.	0.94	0.94	0.44	0.54	0.95	1.13	0.82	0.54	0.37	0.50
10. Receiving oral sex.	1.92	2.33	1.82	1.89	1.86	2.50	1.20	1.62	1.25	2.95
11. Giving oral sex.	1.98	2.37	1.64	1.87	2.02	2.74	1.32	1.87	1.82	2.88

12. Watching others have sex.	1.04	0.75	1.11	0.54	0.98	0.84	0.46	0.23	1.10	0.70
13. Sex with an animal.	0.15	0.07	0.08	0.01	0.05	0.00	0.10	0.01	0.04	0.04
14. Whipping or spanking someone.	1.90	1.23	1.05	0.70	1.17	0.95	0.31	0.17	0.29	0.20
15. Being whipped or spanked.	2.72	2.21	1.44 —	1.14	1.67	1.45	0.70	0.35	0.11	0.22
16. Taking someone's clothes off.	2.12	2.38	1.37	1.50	1.11	2.11	1.32	1.80	1.84	2.88
17. Having your clothes taken off.	2.06	2.12	1.37	1.43	1.06	1.76	1.38	1.59	1.33	2.48
18. Making love elsewhere than bedroom (e.g. kitchen, bathroom).	1.72	1.95	1.60	1.86	1.20	2.05	0.93	1.63	1.49	2.66
19. Being excited by material or clothing (e.g. rubber, leather, underwear).	3.03	2.73	4.44	4.24	4.02	4.18	2.51	2.97	0.80	1.08
20. Hurting a partner.	1.07	0.78	0.55	0.44	0.41	0.50	0.12	0.13	0.12	0.28
21. Being hurt by a partner.	2.07	1.66	1.16	0.99	1.25	1.05	0.47	0.41	0.10	0.24
22. Mate-swapping.	0.73	0.37	0.77	0.23	0.92	0.47	0.51	0.14	0.77	0.26
23. Being aroused by watching someone urinate.	0.71	0.52	0.45	0.40	0.14	0.34	0.12	0.12	0.12	0.22
24. Being tied up.	2.48	2.20	2.14	1.47	2.27	2.18	0.87	0.49	0.18	0.22
25. Tying someone up.	1.80	1.32	1.61	1.06	1.79	1.84	0.38	0.28	0.46	0.32
26. Having incestuous sexual relations.	0.30	0.13	0.31	0.04	0.05	0.05	0.15	0.06	0.10	0.02
27. Exposing yourself provocatively.	0.41	0.32	0.36	0.17	0.23	0.10	0.31	0.20	0.18	0.32
28. Transvestism (wearing clothes of the opposite sex).	1.44	1.37	1.50	1.14	1.01	1.13	3.84	4.63	0.12	0.12

(Continued)

(Continued)

	Sado-masochists F	A	Rubberites F	A	Leatherites F	A	Transvestites F	A	Controls F	A
29. Being promiscuous.	1.21	1.15	0.93	0.78	0.68	0.71	0.93	0.63	1.08	1.18
30. Having sex with someone much younger than yourself.	1.81	1.20	1.71	0.74	0.88	0.50	0.88	0.41	1.46	1.74
31. Having sex with someone much older than yourself.	0.98	0.86	0.77	0.61	0.55	0.50	0.58	0.40	0.66	0.64
32. Being much sought after by the opposite sex.	1.71	1.03	1.39	1.12	1.11	0.84	1.34	0.84	1.21	1.20
33. Being seduced as an "innocent."	1.30	0.54	0.90	0.33	0.71	0.50	0.98	0.30	0.48	0.42
34. Seducing an "innocent."	1.05	0.47	0.81	0.17	0.53	0.32	0.48	0.15	0.92	0.70
35. Being embarrassed by failure of sexual performance.	0.61	1.24	0.45	1.27	0.27	1.21	0.34	1.10	0.36	1.04
36. Having sex with someone of different race.	1.30	0.97	0.91	0.49	1.07	0.61	0.58	0.36	0.94	0.92
37. Using objects for stimulation (e.g. vibrators, candles).	1.34	1.74	1.36	0.43	1.55	1.82	0.63	0.90	0.64	0.88
38. Being masturbated to orgasm by a partner.	2.20	2.69	2.42	2.58	2.03	2.79	1.39	1.99	1.66	2.50
39. Looking at obscene pictures or films.	1.72	2.89	1.49	2.23	1.29	2.26	0.92	1.80	1.10	2.20
40. Kissing passionately.	2.08	3.08	2.12	2.94	1.57	3.34	1.72	3.28	1.63	3.76
Mean (over items)	1.54	1.40	1.29	1.07	1.11	1.32	0.91	0.93	0.87	1.11
F > A	27		27		20		24		16	

might simply mean that the group contains a few more members who are primarily homosexual. One more point before we leave this theme. There are many people who seem to believe that a transvestite is an effeminate homosexual. The figures in fact show that while transvestites may have some homosexual fantasies (really fantasies in which they *as women* make love with men), in terms of performance there is no greater incidence of homosexual activity in the transvestite group than there is in the control group.

Receiving oral sex and *giving oral sex* are much favored by all groups. Oral lovemaking has a curious history, in that although the erotica of the past has always acknowledged its existence, even as late as the 1930s, it was considered slightly unnatural. The Kinsey report (1948) was perhaps the first document to show that it is fairly commonplace. Byrne and Lamberth (1971) found cunnilingus to be the most arousing fantasy among men, group oral sex the second most arousing and fellatio the fourth most arousing theme. Face-to-face intercourse occupied third place. Our findings confirm that among both young and old men, variant and normal groups, oral sex rivals ordinary intercourse in popularity, both as a fantasy and an activity.

Watching others have sex. This theme is of relatively little interest to the transvestites, but otherwise shows no significant differences between groups.

Sex with an animal shows no significant differences between groups and low ratings all around. A minor curiosity is that, in spite of its apparently low popularity, pornographers still produce material of this nature. This could mean that the theme is so socially unacceptable that our subjects were inhibited from expressing any interest, even in spite of their anonymity. Alternatively, it might mean that people are voyeuristically interested in seeing other people have sex with animals while not wanting to have it themselves.

Whipping or spanking someone significantly involves the fetishists as well as the sadomasochists, though, of course, not quite to the same extent. *Being whipped or spanked* is enjoyed in fantasy at a significantly high level by all variant groups; this is true also of reality except for the transvestites. In these two themes we find, of course, an echo both in content and in results of the earlier themes of forcing and being forced.

Taking someone's clothes off and *having one's clothes taken off* are also themes where the spread of results makes interpretation difficult. All that emerges is the sadomasochistic group's significantly higher preference for the latter theme, and if we take notice of relevant pornography, the fantasy is more likely that of being forcibly stripped than of being "romantically" undressed. Notice once more this group's relatively strong interest in the passive version of the theme; as in themes 7 and 8 and 14 and 15, the submissive attitude seems to gain strength in the variant groups compared with controls.

Making love outside the bedroom has, curiously, significantly less appeal to the transvestite group than to the other groups. Perhaps their ideal image of femininity is not as well sustained outside the bedroom. Note that the reality scores on this item are consistently lower for the variant groups, which is a clue to the possibility that they are in some respects more conventional and conforming than the controls.

Being excited by material or clothing naturally shows a massive response from the fetishistic group, but it also rates very significantly higher with the other two variant groups. This is not altogether unexpected, since Benjamin's second category of transvestite is classified as fetishistic, while a sadomasochistic episode is virtually always signaled by—and is often intimately concerned with—the wearing of some costume (nurse, *gauleiter*, schoolboy, maid) symbolizing the role involved.

Hurting a partner appeals especially only to the rubber fetishist and the sadomasochist; *being hurt by a partner* appeals significantly more to all the variant groups. Once again, all the variant groups show a bias toward submission. Some may argue that these two themes make themes 14 and 15 (whipping and spanking) redundant. Many subjects with masochistic inclinations, however, have disagreed with that idea, saying that they find physical beating—even in fantasy—completely unattractive, and that other ways of being hurt are far more pleasant.

Mate-swapping draws no group preferentially. In spite of the amount of attention given in the media (sex-oriented and otherwise) to this particular activity so beloved of the "swinging sixties," it actually has a low rating (less than "seldom") in the fantasies, let alone the behavior, of any of the groups, variant or not. Wilson's previous research (1978) noted that a younger group of males—average age twenty-eight years— showed the same average lack of interest in this theme. Of course, some of our subjects might not have had a mate to swap; but even so the ratings of this item are strikingly low.

Being aroused by watching someone urinate is even more of a minority interest, but seems preferentially to arouse the rubber fetishist and the sadomasochist.

Being tied up is another theme that unites all the variant groups in a significantly greater liking for both fantasy and activity than that shown by the control group. Its counterpart, *tying someone up*, appeals significantly to the sadomasochist and fetishistic groups, but not on average to the transvestite. It is again noticeable that, as before in the paired sadomasochistic themes, it is the submissive version of the fantasy that has the higher appeal to the variant groups (the reverse being the case for the controls).

Having incestuous sexual relations appeals slightly more to the variant groups than to the control group, but the differences are not significant and all the ratings are very low. This is perhaps somewhat surprising in view of the popularity of the seducing "Auntie" who crops up in some specialist sex magazines. Perhaps the word "incest" conjures up images of mothers and sisters rather than the slightly less taboo concept of the older woman who a child often calls "Auntie" even when there is no actual family relationship.

Exposing oneself provocatively again shows higher favor with the variant groups, but the difference is not significant.

Such a theme is, of course, associated more with the female than the male—unless one counts the offense of indecent exposure, which for one reason or another is almost unheard of in women. Anticipating our study of a group of dominant women, the "superbitches," in Chapter 7, we notice that the group rating for this theme among these women is fourteen times as high as the normal male rating.

Wearing clothes of the opposite sex is naturally the prime theme for the transvestites, and the significantly high ratings for the other groups may now come as less of a surprise to the reader in view of our arguments concerning the fetishistic elements in female clothing and the submissive elements in male-to-female cross-dressing (especially "forced" cross-dressing, of course).

Being promiscuous does not appeal significantly any more or less to the variant groups than to the control group. It thus seems that there is little support in our results for the view sometimes expressed that variant behavior leads to promiscuity, or vice versa. In fact, the highest mean score for promiscuous behavior is registered by the control group.

Having sex with someone much younger and *having sex with someone much older* are also themes which individually fail to distinguish between variant and control groups. The higher ratings associated with the first theme are of course to be expected with men in this age group. One can see in the ratio between these two scores (especially the behavior score rather than the fantasy) a tendency for the control group to discriminate more decisively in favor of younger partners; perhaps this also reflects the submissive tendency of the variant groups—younger partners are not so good at dominating in the bedroom.

Being much sought after by the opposite sex is an appealing fantasy to most mature males, as the comparatively high average rating for each group shows, but the theme is significantly more powerful for the sadomasochistic group. A study of the answers from this group to the question posed about "special fantasies that we may have omitted" (see the full Sex Fantasy

Questionnaire in Chapter 2) indicates a possible reason for this; a popular theme is that of being "dominated" by several women at once. This ties in with the fact that the sadomasochists have the highest rating of all the groups on the fantasy of "sex with two other people."

Being seduced as an innocent clearly has some appeal to all the variant groups, but only the sadomasochistic and transvestite groups show significantly higher ratings for this fantasy. *Seducing an innocent* is in general less appealing to the variant groups and significantly less so to the transvestite. Since being seduced is an act of submission, we see again that all the variant groups prefer being seduced while the control males prefer to do the seducing.

Being embarassed by failure of sexual performance is not a fantasy reported significantly more often by any one group. Of course, this item is somewhat different from most of the others which are more likely to be positively desired and sought after. The sadomasochistic group comes nearest to registering a significant preoccupation with this theme; nevertheless, it would take a very special kind of masochist to enjoy observing his own sexual failure. Reports of the actual experience are more interesting since it has often been suggested that those who practice variations are to some extent sexually inadequate. Yet there is only the slightest hint of confirmation for this view in our results—the normals do report less failure than any of the variant groups, but not significantly so in statistical terms.

Having sex with someone of a different race again shows no preferential rating from any one group. The reader may also note that the popular tales of the sexual attractiveness or prowess of, for example, blacks or orientals are only marginally reflected in the fantasies of the subjects we have considered. We have, of course, no way of telling what percentage of our subjects contacted by mail were not white, although we suspect that it is extremely small. This is, perhaps, a subject that merits further research.

Using objects of stimulation appeals particularly to fetishists and sadomasochists (as one might expect) though it is interesting to note that transvestites, a proportion of whom at least are fetishistic, do not regard their items of cross-dressing attire as "objects." The fetishist may or may not do so, but since his fetishistic activities often involve a number of additional "props," the high fantasy rating on this item is not surprising. More difficult to interpret is the low behavior score for the rubber fetishists. One might have expected them to find some stimulation from objects made out of rubber; according to their own reports this does not seem to be true.

Being masturbated to orgasm by a partner. Again being a passive theme, this appeals quite highly to some of the variant groups, especially the rubber fetishists and sadomasochists. Perhaps as a reflection of their generally low libido (which we will discuss shortly), the transvestites score lower than the controls.

Looking at obscene pictures or films produced significantly high scores from the sadomasochists. Perhaps this is because their interest is more readily accommodated in relatively harmless pictorial form. As for the fetishists, many of them felt bound to raise the question: "What do you mean by obscene?" And in so doing they were not hair-splitting; if a picture of a fully dressed girl in a leather or rubber raincoat can be more arousing than one depicting explicit intercourse (a point which we have proved by physiological recording), should we say that the former picture is "more obscene" than the latter? In retrospect, the item might have been better worded "Looking at erotica" rather than using the more subjective concept of obscenity, although of course this might have introduced other difficulties of interpretation.

Kissing passionately. Although no particular group is differentiated by this theme, it is comforting to note that, even in fantasy, so simple a joy as kissing is well above average in popularity for all groups.

So much, then, for our theme-by-theme examination of the Wilson Questionnaire. In previous work, however, it was found by using factor analysis (a statistical technique which puts together those themes which are similarly rated) that the themes discussed can be grouped into four main categories. These are: *intimate* themes such as kissing and intercourse with a loved partner; *exploratory* themes such as mate-swapping, being promiscuous or participating in an orgy; *impersonal* themes such as having sex with a stranger, using objects for stimulation or looking at "obscene" material; and *sadomasochistic* themes like hurting or being hurt by a partner. These classifications were arrived at empirically, that is, by examining how the responses of a randomly collected sample of men and women went together, not on the basis of theory or intuition. When a similar technique was applied to each of the groups studied in this book much the same pattern emerged for the intimate and sadomasochistic themes. The exploratory and impersonal themes were not necessarily as interrelated for the variant groups, but there was little doubt that our subjects' fantasies and probably also their sexual behavior could still be grouped quite usefully under those headings.

If the mean values for the individual themes in each category are therefore added together, we arrive at category ratings for each group, as shown in Table 3. These yield some interesting comparisons: transvestites, for example, show a surprisingly low incidence of intimate fantasies, almost as if such themes, if played out in practice, would lead to conflicts

Table 3. **Mean scores of variant and control groups on four main categories of sexual fantasy derived from the Sex Fantasy Questionnaire.**

	Intimate	Exploratory	Impersonal	Sado-masochistic	Total
Sadomasochists	19.5	11.3	12.8	17.8	61.4
Rubberites	17.4	8.6	13.0	12.8	51.8
Leatherites	15.0	8.7	10.9	13.2	47.8
Transvestites	13.1	7.2	7.4	8.7	36.4
Controls	16.9	8.1	7.6	2.3	34.9

(*Note:* Each category is scored on ten items; see Wilson, 1978, for a list of the items that comprise each factor.)

about their gender identity. But the high incidence of intimate fantasies among the other variant groups counters the often heard suggestion that these groups adopt their deviant practices because they are incapable of, or not interested in, sex within the context of a loving relationship.

The rating differences for exploratory themes are not great enough to distinguish variant from control groups (although the sadomasochists have the highest score in this category), and this may come as a surprise to those who were under the impression that variancy is the hallmark of those at the frontiers of sexual exploration.

The rubber fetishist group scores highest for impersonal themes, as might be expected for a variation that seems at least in some measure to transfer sexual attention from human beings to the inanimate. Interestingly, the leather fetishists are not so clearly distinguished on this factor, although they, and the sadomasochists, are noticeably higher in this category than the control group.

The sadomasochistic fantasy category most strikingly distinguishes all the variant groups from controls—not just the sadomasochists themselves, who of course have the highest score of all. The implication that all the variant groups are preoccupied to a greater-than-average extent with the power elements of sexual relationships—dominance and submission (which may or may not include an interest in physical hurting and being hurt)—is of considerable theoretical interest. If simple avoidance of human relationships were at the root of these variations, they would be distinguished more clearly in the impersonal fantasy category, which might have been sufficient to characterize the fetishists and transvestites, with only the sadomasochists being identified on the sadomasochsm factor.

The fact that the fetishists and transvestites also have sadomasochistic interests could be interpreted as evidence that all our variant groups are alike in seeking particular social relationships for their sexual pleasure. We have already seen that submission is an element that is particularly popular among our variant groups. Are they trying to recall the pleasurable security of infancy as implied by Freudian fixation theory? Do they need an aggressive, dominating partner to initiate sexual activity in order to deal with a problem of guilt? Is it a need to be desired with great lust and passion by someone behaving like an animal rather than a civilized human being? We shall return to the theoretical significance of this finding later in the book.

SEX DRIVE

Table 3 also shows totals for each group for all the fantasy categories. These are of interest because previous work (Wilson, 1978) has shown that total fantasy output is a fairly good indicator of sex drive or libido, if we may borrow the Freudian term. At least this was the case with a representative sample of men (i.e. "normals"), so it is reasonable to suppose that it might also be used to indicate sex drive within our groups of sadomasochists, fetishists and transvestites. Nevertheless, to be sure of this we need to demonstrate that fantasy output relates positively to other recognized criteria of libido such as the number of orgasms per week reported by subjects, the number of partners they have had sex with in their lifetime, and, perhaps best of all, their own estimate of their libido compared with that which they perceive in other people around them. Since each of these measures of libido taken on its own is open to some theoretical criticism, it is probably necessary to look at all of them simultaneously and show that they are positively connected in order to arrive at a satisfactory concept of libido. This in fact was found to be the case; all four measures of libido were in fairly good accord as regards the correlations among them.

The fantasy output scores suggest that the variant groups, especially the sadomasochists, are higher in libido than the controls. Only the transvestites score about the same as normals on total fantasy output. There are, however, reasons for

Table 4. Mean scores (and standard deviations) of variant and control groups on measures of sex drive and satisfaction.

	Sado-masochists	Rubber-ites	Leather-ites	Transvest-ites	Controls
Orgasms					
per week	2.62(1.3)	2.41(1.1)	2.63(1.1)	2.15(1.1)	2.46(1.3)
No. of partners	3.32(1.1)	2.72(0.9)	3.26(1.1)	2.64(0.8)	3.56(1.0)
Self-rated					
libido	3.27(0.9)	3.04(1.0)	3.21(0.8)	2.86(1.0)	3.20(0.9)
Satisfaction					
with partner	2.94(0.9)	3.00(1.1)	3.40(1.4)	3.32(1.0)	3.38(1.1)
Overall sexual					
satisfaction	2.42(1.0)	2.65(1.1)	2.92(1.3)	2.64(1.1)	3.02(1.3)

supposing that these figures may exaggerate the sex drive of the variant groups. We have already seen suggestions in our data (to be confirmed later) that there is a greater discrepancy between fantasy and behavior in the variant groups than in the controls. This is presumably because, as we have said, it is often more difficult to act out variant fantasies than conventional ones. Sadomasochistic fantasies in particular are likely to be difficult to put into practice. Thus, although the correlations among the different sex-drive measures are high, their *levels* do not fully correspond.

When we look at the other indices of sex drive in the Sex Fantasy Questionnaire (Table 4) which are more behavioral and in some ways more direct than the fantasy output measure, we find that all the variant groups have slipped somewhat in relation to the controls, and on one measure—the number of different partners—the controls actually have the highest score. The only really consistent finding is that of low sex drive among the transvestite group, which is what one might expect if a proportion of them were so far toward the transsexual end of the Benjamin classification that they were taking estrogen to consolidate their femininity. Estrogen, the female sex hormone, is known to inhibit the sex drive, and is sometimes even used for treatment of persistent sex offenders because of this property. Alternatively, the transvestite might be modeling himself on the low-libido stereotype of a woman as a means of supporting his female identity.

Overall then, it seems that there is little to distinguish the variant groups from controls with respect to sex drive, although the transvestites seem less sexually active and the other three variant groups have higher levels of fantasy.

In passing we might note again that the number of partners with whom intercourse has been had does not differ greatly from one variant group to another or between variants and controls. All of the variant groups are slightly less experienced than the controls but the difference is not staggering. This finding certainly negates the accusation that people who go in for bizarre sexuality are usually also promiscuous.

Of course, the opposite suggestion has also frequently been made—that some men resort to impersonal and aggressive sexual outlets because they have difficulties with human relationships and in finding partners. On the basis of this idea we might expect the variant groups to be markedly *less* experienced with respect to numbers of sex partners. This is not the case either; they have had a slightly lower range of partners, but this deficiency is not such that we could be justified in calling them "inadequate."

Finally, some people might argue that the variant subjects are half promiscuous and half inadequate, so that these two sections have canceled out and obscured the differences from the normal males. We can tell that this is not true either, for if it were, the dispersion of scores (as indicated in Table 4 by the standard deviation) would be greater for the variant groups than for the controls. Since this is not so, we can be fairly sure that the variant groups are not bimodal as regards number of partners—i.e. they do not naturally subdivide into two extremes.

SATISFACTION

In the past, it was often thought that satisfaction was closely associated with sex drive, that people with high libidos obtain the greatest thrills from sex and those with low libidos feel that they are missing out. The work of Eysenck (1976), however, has shown that libido and satisfaction are fairly independent. One can just as easily be sexually content with no sex drive whatsoever, and very frustrated with a high but unfulfilled libido. Since, as we shall see, there tends to be a greater discrepancy between sexual fantasies (usually the things we would like to do) and sexual behavior (the things we actually do) in the variant groups than in the normal, we might wonder if our variant subjects are less satisifed with their sex lives than other men. The figures in Table 4 show that this is true to some extent.

As regards satisfaction with the partner, the mean ratings of the variant groups are fairly close to those of controls. The sadomasochists and rubber fetishists do seem a little low, though only the sadomasochists are significantly so. It is not surprising that the sadomasochist has more trouble with his partner. Fetishism and transvestism may be carried out without a partner, and in fact, are often preferred that way, so the partner can be assessed on other forms of sexual enjoyment. The sadomasochist, on the other hand, needs a partner for the fulfilment of his desires; seldom can self-bondage or self-flagellation be very effective as a sexual turn-on. If, then, the partner does not participate in the sexual ritual she is likely to be judged adversely. In this connection it is interesting that a survey carried out by Cooperative Motivational Research among their sadomasochistic members revealed that only 17 percent obtained satisfaction of their fantasies at home. The vast majority had to seek outside help, whether professional or otherwise.

But satisfaction with a partner is not the ideal measure for consideration at this point because the variant subjects are more likely to be without steady partners. Whereas 78 percent of our control males claim steady partners, whether married to them or not, this figure is only 57 percent for the sadomasochists and around 65 percent for the other three groups. Therefore, it makes more sense to look at overall sexual satisfaction. Here all the variant groups rate themselves lower than the controls; the difference reaches statistical significance for both sadomasochists and transvestites, with the rubber fetishists very close behind. It appears, then, that the variant subjects, with the exception of the relatively small group of leatherites, are inclined to be less happy and fulfilled in their sex life than the control group. Once again, though, the differences are not staggering, and there is a great deal of overlap between normal and variant groups.

FANTASY VERSUS REALITY

It will be seen from inspection of Table 2 that there is a fair degree of correspondence between the fantasy scores and the activity scores within each group of subjects. The correlation coefficient enables us to quantify this, and we find coefficients ranging between 0.79 and 0.86 for the different groups. This indicates that there is indeed a strong tendency for fantasy and behavior to be related—if we fantasize about something a lot we are also likely to do it a lot. Of course, this tells us nothing about cause and effect, but probably the two interact in a complex way, with fantasies guiding our behavior on some occasions while at other times our fantasies are inspired by memories of pleasant experiences in the recent or distant past.

But how can we tell which groups are most successful in fulfilling their fantasies? Comparing the correlations for the different groups is not helpful because the fetishists and transvestites have one overwhelming theme that they both think about and practice a lot, while the other groups have more scattered preferences. If, however, we plot the fantasy scores against the activity scores for each theme within a particular group, and then draw a straight line through all these points, we do discover differences among the various groups. In Figure 1 the activity scores are on the upright and fantasy scores on the perpendicular, so the steeper the rise of the line the more reality-oriented or "fulfilled" the group is inclined to be. The control males seem best able to put their fantasies into practice and the sadomasochists least so, which is just what our findings concerning sexual satisfaction would lead us to expect. Note that this result also fits with another, perhaps simpler, method of calculating the discrepancy between fantasy and reality shown in the bottom line of Table 2: a simple count of the number of themes in the questionnaire on which the fantasy received higher ratings than the reality. The controls rated the fantasy higher on only sixteen items, while for the sadomasochists and rubberites, fantasy exceeded activity on twenty-seven items.

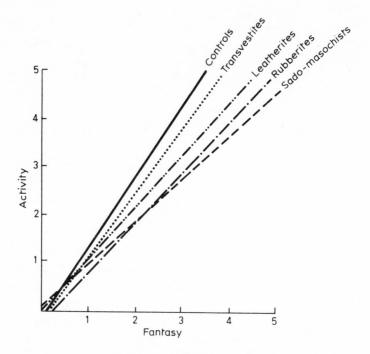

Figure 1. The relationship between fantasy and activity in control and variant groups. These regression lines are drawn through the fantasy/activity scattergrams for each group: it can be seen that the control group translates fantasy into activity with greater ease than the variant groups; sadomasochists, as might be expected, have the greatest difficulty of all the groups.

Yet we should not get too carried away by these differences between the groups just because they confirm our theoretical expectations. They are in fact fairly small differences and, in the case of the transvestites and fetishists in particular, they arise out of discrepancies occurring in themes that are fairly well down the hierarchy of preferences. As far as their prime preoccupations are concerned (cross-dressing and being turned on by materials) the reality scores are well up beside those of the fantasy.

We should also at this point introduce some of the problems that will be addressed in the final chapter. In particular, we must consider whether some of the activities of our variant groups should not themselves be classified as fantasies— albeit fantasies supported by physical role-playing. When, for example, a sadomasochist is acting out a whipping scenario with a woman in high-heeled boots, we have probably only reached a second-order level of fantasy. What is optimally exciting to this man is probably his approximation of some other more intense experience which is less feasible. How would it feel to be whipped *really hard* rather than just playfully? What would it have been like to have been Cleopatra's slave in the days of ancient Egypt? When a transvestite dresses as a woman, it may be to sharpen his fantasy of what it is like to be a woman having sex, or being the focus of admiring attention. The rubber fetishist? Who knows? He may be trying to reconstruct a springy, secure, womblike world. And so on. Are these behaviors in themselves the ultimate, or are they approximations to it? And if the latter, should we call them activities or fantasies? Somehow they seem less "finished" than the fulfilling of a desire for someone by having conventional intercourse with him or her. What is certain is that the boundaries between fantasy and reality are not always well defined.

SIMILARITIES AMONG THE GROUPS

So far we have concentrated on the ways in which our variant and normal groups may be distinguished from one another.

But it will not have escaped the astute reader that some of the variant groups also have a lot in common. Many of the masochist themes, such as being forced, tied, whipped and spanked, distinguish all the variant groups from our male controls. So, too, do the fetishistic and transvestite items. Thus our fetishists often tend to be sadomasochistic and transvestite, our transvestites tend to be fetishistic and sadomasochistic, and our sadomasochists tend also to be fetishistic and transvestite. Are these groups, then, so close in their sexual predilections that they could be merged together and treated as one? Is it the case that "a variation by any other name is equal fun"?

Figure 2 is derived from the correlations among the sexual activities of the different groups and shows how closely each is related to the other. From this it can be seen that the leatherites are virtually indistinguishable from the sadomasochists with respect to sexual behavior and the rubberites are also very close. The transvestites fall quite a bit further away from these three variant groups and, incidentally, closer to the control males. The transsexuals are "beyond" the transvestites, going further away from both the sadomaso-fetishists and the normals. It is a pity that this analysis was conducted before a suitable female control group was available for inclusion, though we could expect it to fall nearest to the transsexuals at the top of the diagram.

These results imply that it was almost accidental whether some of our subjects were contacted through rubber, leather or sadomasochistic organizations. Many of them, it seems, would be just about as well suited by the other two groups. Nevertheless, despite this apparent near-identity among them, we shall continue to treat them separately in the analyses that follow because certain differences, other than actual sexual behavior, may account for their particular affiliation, and the detailed differences among them may be illuminating. Thus, we have already seen that the levels of fantasy, libido and satisfaction are slightly different from one group to another. We shall also note differences in personality and social background in the chapters to follow.

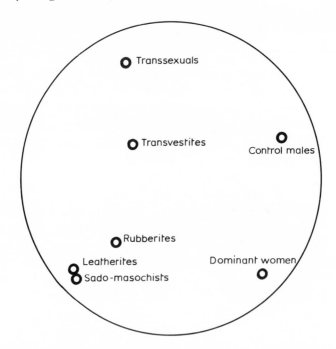

Figure 2. A similarity space analysis of variant and control groups based on the intercorrelations in sexual behavior patterns. The shorter the distance between groups, the more alike they are in terms of sexual preferences.

The distinction between the rubberites and leatherites is of particular theoretical interest because it may provide clues as to critical learning experiences involved in fetishistic attachments. Actually, there was a great deal of overlap between these two fetish targets with a high proportion of leatherites claiming an equally strong interest in rubber. Unfortunately, we did not have data going the other way, but our interview experience suggests that many rubberites are also attracted by leather. But that one material dominates the other is indicated by a negative correlation between them; the more attracted a leatherite was to leather the less interest he expressed in rubber and vice versa (correlation = −0.45). So what determines the preferred choice of material?

There are only two individual themes on the Sex Fantasy Questionnaire that significantly distinguish the rubberites and leatherites. These are urination and incest, both of which occur more often in the rubberites. A field day for the psychoanalysts: despite the distaste usually voiced by rubberites to the idea, could the urination interest support the idea that the origins of their predilection date back to infantile wetting of rubber sheets or baby pants? Robert Stoller's idea that a variant fantasy expresses an infant trauma in more pleasurable or triumphant form seems to be particularly persuasive in this instance. The sudden decline in rubberites born after the Second World War that is detectable in Figure 6, Chapter 6, might also seem to support this infantile origin theory. For a possible explanation of this statistic, see page 127.

Why do the rubberites have more incest fantasies than the leatherites? Is it an expression of a desire to return to the womb of the mother? Is it, again, a fixation on the mother, older sister or "seducing Auntie" who changed the rubber sheets and pants in infancy? Such psychodynamic excursions are not really warranted on the basis of the slender fantasy differences observed in our questionnaire, especially since the sadomasochists are even more interested in urination than the rubberites and show the same difference from the leatherites on the incest fantasy.

Our similarity space analysis shows that the transvestites are clearly separable from the fetishist and sadomasochist groups in terms of sexual behavior. This is perhaps not surprising when it is considered that the Beaumont Society (from whom our transvestites were obtained) tends to discourage the more fetishistically oriented transvestite from joining, and instead shows a preference for the "true" transvestite of Benjamin's classification.

We did not know, however, whether the two types were entirely separate, so two additional questions were asked of this group, designed to discover, first, to what extent cross-dressing was done in order to achieve sexual arousal and, second, to what extent it was done because the subject wished to belong (or felt he did belong) to the opposite sex. As far as we can judge, most previous researchers asked these two questions in one—"Do you cross-dress to feel sexy *or* because you think you are like a woman?" The possibility that both might occur at once seems to have been little explored. The present data shows that cross-dressing in this Society at least occurs partly to obtain arousal (rating 2.67, where 2 = "only a bit," 3 = "partly") but more because the subject wished that he belonged, or felt he did belong, to the opposite sex (rating 3.60, where 3 = "partly," 4 = "mostly"). True, the higher the arousal impulse was, the lower was the feeling of "being" a woman (correlation −0.32); nevertheless, examination of the individual results rather than the trends alone showed plenty of cases in which both impulses occurred simultaneously.

It appears, then, that there is some overlap between our transvestites and fetishists, but not enough that the groups cannot be treated as synonymous. Likewise, as we shall see, the transvestites have a lot in common with the transsexuals, who are mostly, of course, drawn from the same club membership. But the transsexual differs from the transvestite in the opposite direction from the fetishist. So it seems that a straight line drawn from the sadomasochists to the transsexuals in Figure 2 would represent the Benjamin classification of transvestites fairly accurately, with those in the middle of the continuum being most unequivocally deserving of that label.

SADISM VERSUS MASOCHISM

We also wondered to what extent it might be profitable to split our sadomasochists into those who were predominantly sadistic and those with primarily masochistic leanings. Within a group of normal males, Wilson (1978) had found such a close connection between sadistic and masochistic inclinations that he recommended scoring the Sex Fantasy Questionnaire on a joint factor of sadomasochism. It does not, of course, follow that within specialist groups such as those we are studying it is necessarily unprofitable to seek a distinction between sadism and masochism.

We did this by scoring each subject in the sadomasochistic group separately for sadism (sum of scores for forcing, whipping, hurting and tying up) and masochism (sum of scores for being forced, being whipped, being hurt and being tied up). If the sadism score was higher than the masochism score we called that individual a "sadist," and if the masochism score was higher than the sadism score we called the man a "masochist." This admittedly arbitrary classification yielded two subgroups of ninety-one masochists and thirty-seven sadists, confirming our earlier observation of the masochistic preference.

We were somewhat surprised to discover no differences between these two groups in terms of libido or sexual satisfaction. As we shall see in the next chapter, however, there were some slight differences in personality. The sadists emerged as slightly tougher, more extraverted and less neurotic—just as we might have expected, an altogether more masculine personality profile.

When average sadism and masochism scores based on the same selection of fantasy items were calculated for each group of subjects and plotted in relation to total fantasy output, the results in Figure 3 were obtained. The controls showed little in the way of either type of fantasy (as we have already observed in Table 3) but the sadistic fantasies that they did report outnumbered those that were masochistic. All of the variant groups, however, showed the reverse pattern, with masochistic fantasies outnumbering the sadistic. This was a tendency that we had noted in our earlier theme-by-theme analysis of the Sex Fantasy Questionnaire, and is perhaps the prime way in which the variant groups are distinguishable from the controls. Members of the variant groups seem quite eager to "take their punishment like a man"—but preferably from a woman.

Since there was a hint in this graph that groups with a higher production of fantasy are relatively more interested in

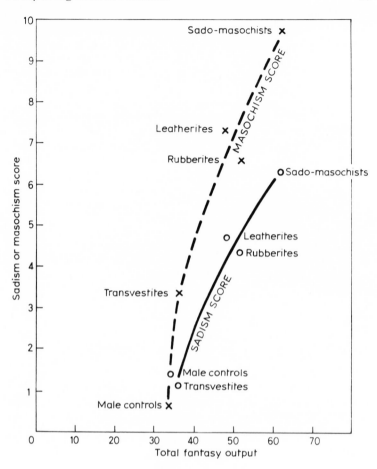

Figure 3. Sadism and masochism scores of variant and control groups plotted in relation to total fantasy output. Both masochistic (or submissive) fantasies and sadistic (or aggressive) fantasies increase as total fantasy output increases, but the former increase faster than the latter.

masochistic than sadistic fantasies, we decided to see whether there is a tendency within these groups for masochistic fantasies to grow at a faster rate than sadistic fantasies as the total output of fantasy, and presumably also the sex drive, increases. In Figure 4 we have some confirmation of this hy-

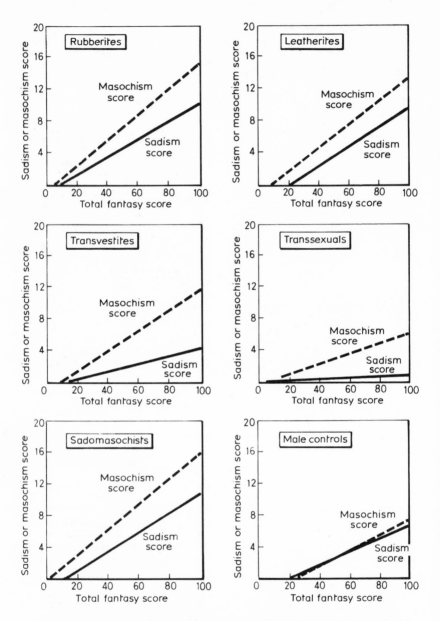

Figure 4. Sadism and masochism scores related to total fantasy output within each male group, variant and control. Each line is a line of best fit through the appropriate scattergram. Note that the masochistic or submissive fantasies increase in frequency faster than do sadistic or aggressive fantasies as total fantasy output rises (see also Figure 8).

pothesis. In each group the regression line (computer-drawn through the scattergrams) is steeper for the masochism score than the sadism score. This is most noticeable in the transvestites but the consistency across the other groups, including the controls, is very impressive.

At first glance, it might seem strange that the controls show such a similar pattern to the two groups of fetishists, which are, of course, very much like one another, but it must be remembered that the majority of control subjects lie toward the bottom left of the graph, in the area where sadism is higher than masochism. In one sense they are like the sadomasochists, who also show a greater sadistic predilection until higher overall levels of fantasy are attained, but the crossover for this latter group occurs at a higher fantasy level where, coincidentally, the majority of sadomasochists are located.

But why should it be the case that high fantasy scores are more likely to be composed of masochistic themes than sadistic? A possible interpretation of this fact in terms of the sociobiology of sex and aggression will be suggested in the final chapter of the book. In the meantime, we will proceed to look at some of the other differences among our groups.

5

Personality and Mental Health

In the last chapter we looked at the patterns of sexual fantasy and behavior that characterize our variant groups, and the way in which they are distinguished from one another and from "normal" in these respects. We now consult our data derived from the *Eysenck Personality Questionnaire* to discover how, if at all, our groups can be identified in terms of temperament, stability and happiness in life.

Such an exercise is of interest to the psychologist because the findings may be expected to bear on several theories of the origin of sexual preferences, especially those traditionally designated as deviant, and to help us to choose between them or perhaps discard them altogether. We shall discuss the theoretical implications of our results as we come to them, and again in the final chapter. In the meantime it will be helpful to the reader to have a little background to some of these theories.

In Chapter 2 we described the three dimensions measured by the *Eysenck Personality Inventory*—psychoticism (or tough-mindedness), neuroticism (or emotionality) and extraversion (versus introversion). Eysenck's theory would suppose that each of these dimensions would be implicated to some extent in the genesis of sexual behavior patterns, and this he has demonstrated (at least in the realm of "normal" people) in his book *Sex and Personality* (1976). Extraverts are found to be characteristically outgoing, sociable and novelty-seeking in their sexual behavior, as though they are trying to offset painful boredom (low cortical arousal in Eysenck's theory) with plenty of activity, excitement and social contact. They have intercourse more often than introverts, with more partners and in a greater variety of positions. Introverts are relatively shy and inexperienced in all these respects.

Many theorists have supposed that sexual deviates have acquired their unusual interests because of difficulties in social interaction, particularly with adult members of the opposite sex. The assumption is that an oblique sex object (for instance, leather boots, cruelty, women's clothing, perhaps even animals, children or members of the same sex) has been adopted because the individual is in some sense socially inadequate. Perhaps he lacks the skills or physical good looks with which to attract members of the opposite sex. Perhaps he has had some unfortunate early experience with potential sex partners: hostility, rejection or humiliation. Again, perhaps his experiences with adults during his upbringing were so painful that he acquired an attitude toward one or both sexes that is detrimental to sexual relationships. These are interesting ideas which seem plausible but have so far received little empirical support. They share the prediction that people with variant sex patterns will be introverted in personality.

Eysenck himself has another reason for expecting that people with variant sexuality are more likely to be introverted. According to his theory, introverts have a higher level of arousal in their cerebral cortex which lends itself more readily to conditioned emotional fixations, including phobias and obsessions as well as idiosyncratic sexual attachments. Thus in Eysenck's theory, introverts are both more likely to be affected by guilt and conscience, with consequent risk to their sexual development, and more likely positively to imprint their sexual interest in a relatively accidental way. Of course, if we were to find that our variant groups were not noticeably more introverted than controls, then all these theoretical explanations would be irrelevant.

Predictions concerning neuroticism are much less clear. We would expect people with variant sex interests who are confused, anxious, guilty or otherwise unhappy with their predilection to be higher in neuroticism than controls, but there is a classic problem of cause and effect here. We do not know whether the general predisposition toward anxiety and conflict leads to the sexual difficulties, or whether the unusual sexual predilection gives rise to the "neurotic" worries. It could even be the perception of social censure rather than the simple fact of the variant behavior that gives rise to the anxieties. There are problems in inferring the direction of cause and effect with virtually all the correlations we have to report, but none are so problematic as those at this particular point.

There is one slightly less ambiguous prediction we could make with respect to the neuroticism factor. Women, in line with their well-known stereotype, come out as rather more emotional than men in this dimension. Therefore, if our transvestites and transsexuals have personalities tending toward those of women, or if they are simulating the attitudes and emotions of women, we expect them to score higher on the neuroticism scale than normal men. Again, the prediction is clear even if the mechanism by which we expect it to emerge is not.

By contrast, the psychoticism factor is known to be associated with masculinity. Men in general score higher than women on this scale, and men with an aggressive, "macho" nature score higher still. Thus if our transvestites and transsexuals are gentle and feminine in personality, we expect them to be more in the range of normal women than normal men in this dimension. The position of the other groups on the psychoticism scale is more difficult to predict, although we might suppose that sadomasochists with a sadistic orientation would be higher on the scale—i.e. tougher—than those with a masochistic orientation. Also, we might expect that leatherites, because of the sadistic connotation of their favorite material, would be higher on the psychoticism scale than rubberites. (Unfortunately, we have no fur or silk fetishists with whom to compare these groups because we would expect them to be even more feminine and perhaps more like the transvestites.)

Apart from comparing our variant groups with normal males and females it is interesting to see how they compare with certain clinical groups such as schizophrenics, psychopaths and obsessive-compulsive neurotics. This is because many people—medical professionals as well as laypersons—have suggested that our groups should be classified with these clinical groups. Thus they might argue that the transvestite is just plain crazy and should be in a mental institution along with all the other schizophrenics. The sadomasochist, they might suppose, is just a psychopath who happens to specialize in the area of sex rather than straightforward assault and battery, theft or embezzlement. The fetishist they might think of as a special kind of obsessive-compulsive neurotic. It will therefore be enlightening to consider how our sexual groups compare, on the psychoticism and neuroticism dimensions in particular, with the scores obtained from certain clinical samples. This will enable us to assess the overall degree, if any, of pathology that exists in these groups and will give us a clue as to whether many of their members are in need of medical care.

First, we shall examine the mean scores for the variant groups that are shown in Table 5. For the more visually inclined reader some of this data is also depicted in Figure 5.

In line with the hypotheses outlined above, the sadomasochistic men are slightly more introverted and neurotic than the control males. The differences, however, are not so great as to allow us to conclude that social inadequacy is a sufficient explanation of the sadomasochist's unusual sexual proclivities.

The psychoticism score of the sadomasochists is also

Table 5. **Mean scores (and standard deviations) of variant and normal groups on personality factors measured by the** *Eysenck Personality Questionnaire.*

	No. in Group	Extra-version	Neuroti-cism	Psychoti-cism	Lie scale
Sadomasochists	133	10.68(5.3)	11.03(5.9)	3.50(3.0)	7.92(4.2)
Rubberites	87	10.87(—)	10.49(—)	— (—)	8.91(—)
Leatherites	38	12.55(4.6)	9.94(5.9)	3.29(1.9)	9.87(4.6)
Transvestites	269	9.96(5.4)	13.27(5.8)	3.27(2.3)	8.32(4.2)
Transsexuals	16	9.50(5.2)	13.06(5.5)	3.19(2.3)	11.12(4.2)
Dominant women	25	14.04(5.5)	12.68(4.5)	5.92(3.8)	7.00(4.4)
Control Males[1]	50	12.38(5.1)	9.17(5.1)	3.09(2.6)	8.07(4.1)
Control Females (1)[2]	416	12.24(4.9)	12.63(5.4)	2.35(2.1)	8.86(3.9)
Control Females (2)[3]	27	11.97(5.0)	12.57(5.3)	2.28(2.2)	8.84(4.1)

Notes
1. Control males are matched in age and social class with male variant groups.
2. This group of females is age-matched with the various male groups from *E.P.Q.* standardization data.
3. These control females were collected specifically for our study and are age-matched for comparison specifically with the dominant women (Superbitches).

slightly elevated in line with the suggestion that this group is fairly high in libido. It should be remembered that psychoticism is thought to have something to do with the effects of androgen, the male sex hormone, which of course increases the sex drive in both men and women.

What happens when we split the sadomasochistic group into two: those who specialize in sadism and those whose prime interest is masochistic? The findings are shown in Table 6.

We had expected the sadists to be markedly higher than the masochists on the psychoticism dimension. In fact, the difference between them in this respect is very slight and insignificant. There is also little difference with respect to neuroticism. Only on the extraversion factor is there any notable difference—the masochists being more introverted than the sadists. What this reveals is that the sadistic subgroup is

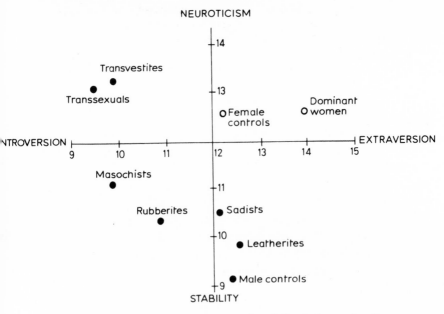

Figure 5. The position of various groups in relation to two major dimensions of personality.

about the same as the control males with regard to introversion-extraversion, while the masochists, as a group, are significantly introverted. Why this should be the case is not immediately clear, except that insofar as punishment is accepted by a conscience as expiation for sins real or imagined, the introverted masochist might welcome it more because, according to Eysenck's personality theory, he would have acquired a stronger conscience.

The personality information on the rubberites was mostly collected in an earlier study by Gosselin (1979). Unfortunately, a different version of the *Eysenck Personality Questionnaire* was used which did not incorporate a psychoticism scale. Also, since the items in the other scales were slightly different, we have been able to compute equivalent mean scores, but the standard deviations have been omitted because we cannot be sure of their comparability. Still, such informa-

Table 6. **Mean scores (and standard deviations) on Eysenck personality dimensions of sadomasochists, divided into those who are primarily sadistic and those who are primarily masochistic.**

	No. in group	Extraversion	Neuroticism	Psychoticism
Sadists	37	12.05(4.9)	10.51(7.3)	3.75(3.5)
Masochists	91	9.97(5.3)	11.26(5.3)	3.34(2.6)

tion as we have on the rubberites indicates that they are similar to the sadomasochists in personality, being slightly introverted and emotional compared with the control males (though neither variant group approaches the level of emotionality of the control women). As with the sadomasochists, the lie scale score for the rubberites is unexceptional.

The leatherites, surprisingly perhaps, are virtually indistinguishable from the male control group. Admittedly, they are smaller in number than either of the two previous groups, which makes our finding a little less reliable; even so, one might have expected on the basis of the sex-pattern data to find them more similar to the sadomasochists and rubberites. So often in psychological research we think we see a clear pattern beginning to emerge, only to experience disappointment when later findings fail to conform with and confirm that trend.

Next we consider the transvestites, our largest variant group, with 269 members. Here we find clear evidence of introversion and high neuroticism compared with normal males (though only slightly higher than the female controls). The psychoticism and lie scores are again unexceptional. So transvestites are not in the least crazy, as some people might think, but they do seem to be socially reserved and rather emotional.

Here, of course, we have a problem of interpretation. Our transvestites may have adopted an impersonal source of sexual satisfaction because they were shy and withdrawn socially, or they may have isolated themselves following the development of their predilection (which they are no doubt aware is often greeted in society with hostility and derision). Their high level of emotionality could be partly at the root of their female interest and identification, or it could be a deliberate attempt on the part of some transvestites to simulate the female stereotype in their *E.P.Q.* responses. We do not really have the data to decide between these alternative explanations; nevertheless, it is interesting to note that our results are consistent with the theoretical expectations outlined above. To our knowledge this much has not been demonstrated before.

If we were to guess the direction of cause and effect operating here we would probably be inclined to think that the temperamental characteristics preceded the development of the sexual preferences. There is a fair amount of evidence available now to support the idea that the Eysenck personality dimensions are stable, biologically determined traits which are not very sensitive to life experiences. Although neurotic introversion in itself is not a direct or sufficient cause of transvestism, or any other sexual variation, the present findings suggest that constitutional factors of temperament probably predispose or contribute to the development of unconventional sex patterns.

The transsexuals and dominant women are fairly small in number, and Chapter 7 is devoted to a discussion of their characteristics. It is sufficient to note at this stage that the transsexuals seem just like their Beaumont Society associates, the transvestites, in personality (being introverted and emotional compared with normal males) while the dominant women (or "Superbitches" as they sometimes call themselves) are very tough-minded and rather extraverted compared with normal women.

Actually, the dominant women are so high on the psychoticism scale as to be comparable with male psychotics, prisoners and patients with personality disorders (Table 7). They are thus very exceptional in this regard, but we still hesitate to suggest that they are clinically abnormal or "pathological" because high psychoticism scores (like high libido scores) can occur for a variety of different reasons. Their very high libido,

eccentricity and disregard for social convention may be sufficient to elevate their psychoticism scores to this level without
there being any significant amount of thought disorder or
criminal impulse. This remains to be seen, of course, but a
personality score by itself should never be used as an indict-
ment—other, more direct evidence of pathology should be
awaited. Some clinicians might call these dominant women
nymphomaniacs, especially since so many of them derive intense enjoyment from their activities, but we consider this to
be moralistic and outmoded.

Note that the psychoticism score of the dominant women is
the only one of clinical proportion. None of the male variant
groups show personality profiles that are comparable to those
of the psychotics, neurotics or criminals shown in Table 7.
Even patients with assorted sex problems have significantly
higher psychoticism scores than any of our male variants.

Incidentally, we should consider whether any of these personality patterns could be affected by the way in which our
samples were obtained. Could the fact that they have all
joined clubs have some bearing on the nature of their personality profiles? Is it possible that individuals with these predilections who are worried about themselves would be more
likely to join a group for comfort and reassurance than those
who are happy and contented? Such self-selection might have
contributed to the slightly elevated neuroticism scores that
are seen in most of our samples. Their tendency toward intro-

**Table 7. Mean personality scores of various clinical groups.
(From _E.P.Q._ standardization data).**

	Extraversion	Neuroticism	Psychoticism	Lie scale
Psychotics (mainly				
schizophrenics)	10.67	13.39	5.66	9.62
Mixed neurotics	9.42	16.56	4.19	8.01
Prisoners	13.62	13.13	5.72	6.78
Personality				
disorders	10.09	15.71	5.78	7.06
Patients with sex				
problems	11.91	12.43	4.87	7.07

Table 8. Correlations of key fantasy items with Eysenck personality dimensions for all variant male groups combined.

	Extraversion	Neuroticism	Psychoticism	Lie scale
Whipping or spanking	0.05	—0.04	0.08	—0.13*
Being whipped or spanked	—0.03	0.03	0.03	—0.06
Being excited by material or clothing	0.14*	—0.01	0.07	—0.13*
Wearing clothes of the opposite sex	—0.08	0.14*	—0.06	—0.06

(*p <.01, i.e. for the starred numbers the odds are less than one in a hundred that these are chance findings.)

version, however, could not be so readily accounted for in this way, since joining a club is a sociable act that we would expect to be more characteristic of the extravert.

Another limitation of using group membership to define our variations is the overlap among them that we have established in Chapter 4. This reduces the power of our analyses, particularly if there are also some fetishists and sadomasochists in our control group, as there well may be. A way of looking at our results which bypasses this problem is to use the ratings on key items in the Sex Fantasy Questionnaire as criteria for the three main variations in which we are interested and see how these relate to personality.

The results of this analysis shown in Table 8 are something of a disappointment. Relationships between personality and the major predilections are very small (although with 453 subjects in the analysis several of them do achieve statistical significance). Subjects with high ratings on the fetishism theme are more likely to be extraverted than those with low ratings, and subjects with high ratings on the transvestism theme are more likely to be neurotic. The tendency for those interested in sadism to be higher on psychoticism just fails to reach significance. There is also a tendency for the fantasy reports, particularly those relating to sadism and fetishism, to go with high lie scores, which is what we might expect if a desire to appear respectable inhibits the declaration of sexual fantasies.

In case these results seem contradictory in relation to our previous analysis of the mean personality scores of the various groups, it should be pointed out that we only calculated these correlations within the groups of variant males. This was because most of our control data came from the *E.P.Q.* standardization, and was therefore not available for this analysis, and the female groups were excluded because we did not feel that they were directly comparable for this purpose. Thus, if we look at the position of the male variant groups alone in Figure 5, we see that the fetishists are indeed toward the extravert side of the diagram (relative to masochists and transvestites) and the transvestites are highest in neuroticism. All that is surprising, then, is how small these personality connections seem to be when based on correlations with individual themes across the groups.

So far we have found little to suggest that our male variant groups are pathological, even allowing that this medical term has any place in psychology. But perhaps a more finely focused approach to our data would be more revealing. Table 9 shows an analysis of nine particular items chosen from the *E.P.Q.* because of their special theoretical interest. Percentages of "yes" answers to these questions are given for each of the variant groups as well as for control samples taken from the *E.P.Q.* standardization. Unfortunately, it was not possible to retrieve this information for the rubberites: fetishism in this case has to be represented by the leatherites alone. Note that these special items were chosen from the full eighty-eight on an *a priori* basis; they were not selected because they were the most powerful discriminators in the test.

The first two items, relating to shyness and sensitivity, were chosen because they are especially pertinent to the hypothesis of social difficulty among the variant groups. The pattern of responses across the different groups is fairly similar for these two: compared with controls, the leatherites and dominant women tend to deny those difficulties, while the sadomasochists, transvestites and transsexuals are more likely to declare them. This supports, in the main, our finding of

Table 9. Responses of variant and normal groups to certain selected items from the *Eysenck Personality Questionnaire.*

Percentage "Yes" responses.

Theoretical factor	Item	Sadomasochists	Leatherites	Transvestites	Transsexuals	Dominant women	Male controls
Shyness	"Do you tend to keep in the background on social occasions?"	70	11	64	69	20	51
Sensitivity	"Are your feelings easily hurt?"	73	11	78	88	16	43
Loneliness	"Do you often feel lonely?"	54	45	51	57	76	29
Depression	"Have you ever wished that you were dead?"	30	31	43	63	52	18
Guilt	"Are you often troubled by feelings of guilt?"	48	29	62	44	52	44
Obsessionality	"Do good manners and cleanliness matter much to you?"	92	63	94	88	72	95
Concern with looks	"Do you worry a lot about your looks?"	36	42	57	82	48	37
Sense of humor	"Do you like telling jokes and funny stories to your friends?"	60	21	58	25	44	80
Relationship with mother	"Is (or was) your mother a good woman?"	93	37	83	100	48	95

Note: Control data are taken from the *E.P.Q.* standardization. Although matched for mean age, there is slightly less variance in the ages of the control males.

greater social introversion in the male variant groups. Of course, the leatherites are a clear exception, and it is surprising in a way that they did not come out as more extraverted overall. Very probably the rubberites would respond in a manner more similar to the sadomasochists.

The next two items, loneliness and depression (or perhaps more correctly "despair") may also be treated as a pair since they produce a similar pattern of results. All the variant groups show a higher proportion of members reporting problems of

this kind than the controls. The dominant women are particularly likely to be lonely (76 percent) and 63 percent of the
transsexuals have "sometimes wished they were dead" compared with only 18 percent of the controls. These figures suggest that a certain amount of unhappiness prevails in the lives
of our sexually unusual people. Whether this unhappiness is
an inevitable concomitant of their way of life or a reaction to
the unpleasant reception accorded to them by society at large
is of course a question that we cannot answer at present. Probably there is always a certain amount of stress involved in
maintaining a minority position in society, but that is not to
say that people in such a position can easily improve their lot
by attempting to conform to the majority. Left-handers have
difficulties because so many instruments are manufactured for
right-hand use, but changing to primary use of the right hand
is seldom a practical solution to that problem.

The items referring to guilt and obsessionality are not very
revealing. The variant groups do not display particularly high
guilt levels: the transvestites with 62 percent are slightly more
likely to be troubled by feelings of guilt than the controls with
44 percent, but on the other hand, the leatherites are less
prone to guilt, with only 29 percent endorsing this item. The
obsessionality item fails as a useful index because 95 percent
of the controls endorse it and, although the variant groups
appear to show less obsessionality, it is doubtful that this comparison is very meaningful.

Concern with looks was investigated as part of the hypothesis of social difficulty. Some theorists have suggested that
perceiving oneself as unattractive (whether or not this is ob-
jectively so) could reduce one's chances of finding a mate and
thus promote impersonal sexual channels. This idea is not
supported in our results, however. The only groups to show
excessive concern with their looks are the transvestites and
transsexuals, and the reasons for this are probably very different from those implied above. These men are no doubt concerned either because their masculine looks do not
correspond with their female feelings or they are worried

about how well they are presenting themselves as women. At any rate, these results cannot be held to provide support for the idea that simple physical unattractiveness is at the root of the sexual variations we have been investigating.

Interest in the item referring to "jokes and funny stories" was inspired by the clinical impression of the authors that many of our variant subjects seemed to take themselves and the world rather seriously; we thus wondered if the groups might be distinguishable on the basis of the role that humor plays in their lives. "Sense of humor" is notoriously difficult to measure, but it seemed to us that a start would be made by examining the self-rating of interest in initiating humor provided by this particular item in the *E.P.Q.* In fact, it is fairly clear that the variant groups do endorse this item less than controls. The leatherites and transsexuals are particularly unlikely to claim a liking for telling jokes and funny stories, only 21 percent and 25 percent respectively agreeing with the statement compared with 80 percent of the controls. We hesitate to leap to any conclusions on the basis of answers to this one question but this finding is quite new as far as we are aware, and it points to an interesting avenue for further research. At present all we can say is that insofar as humor is another marker of positive mental health, the variant groups emerge again as slightly sadder than controls.

The final item that we have picked out for detailed analysis has fairly obvious prominence within psychological theory. Nearly all behavior problems have at one time or another been attributed to a lack of motherly love, and so it is impossible to pass over the opportunity of seeing how our variant groups perceive their mothers. Again we have an item that almost hits the ceiling, with 95 percent of control males evaluating their mother as "a good woman," but the transsexuals show even greater devotion with a 100 percent favorable vote for mother. What a pity the *E.P.Q.* does not solicit a comment on "father," for we might find the transsexuals to be much less unanimous. A committed Freudian might suggest that the transsexual has taken the Oedipus complex one step further—he doesn't want to sleep with mother, he wants to *become* her. Of course, we must resist such excesses and point out that the transsexuals are only slightly more unanimous than the controls in loving their mother.

How do the other groups feel about mother? The sadomasochists are similar to the controls with 93 percent "good," and the transvestites turn in a fairly respectful 83 percent. But once again, we find the leatherites agreeing with the dominant women—less than half of these groups perceive their mother as a good woman.

Just what meaning can be attached to these differential opinions of mother is an open matter for speculation. Many theorists have supposed that men create several images of women which may be incompatible with each other: the moral guardian, the pedestal goddess, the sinful sex object and the nurturant comforter, for instance. Mother may be identified with some of these "ideal" types and not others, and experiences with her may influence attitudes toward these stereotyped images of women. But the precise mechanics, or "dynamics," involved are complex because they can vary from one individual to another and from one time of life to another. For some men, respect for a woman may be a necessary condition of making love to her; to others it may be antithetical. Some men may only be able to have sex with women who evoke no motherly associations whatsoever; others may need a mother figure to instruct or compel them before sexual arousal is possible. We cannot help agreeing with the psychoanalysts that relationships with parents, particularly the mother in the case of the man, are powerful antecedents of adult sexual preferences, and we can only lament our present state of ignorance concerning the details of these effects. There is, however, more evidence relevant to the question of environmental and upbringing influences in the next chapter.

6

Family Background and Upbringing

People very seldom do anything for absolutely no reason at all; there is always a cause, a reason why. Reasons why take two forms: either the person has had a tendency to act in such-and-such a way because that's the way they were born, or else they do what they do because they have learned to do it. Which of these has the greater influence on the eventual mode of thought or action has caused many squabbles both in the world of psychology and in the world around us; the two attitudes have crystallized in the contradictory proverbs "The leopard can't change his spots" and "Constant dripping wears away the stone."

In all areas of behavior both genes and environment are important. Only the fool maintains that one or the other is the sole determinant. Nevertheless, it remains worthwhile to try to establish just how important the genetic factors are relative to environmental factors, and which aspects of the environment are the most important. Unfortunately, there is very little evidence concerning the role of heredity in determining the sexual variations with which we have been dealing.

The classic method for assessing the strength of genetic factors is to look at the similarity of identical and fraternal twins. Identical twins have the same genes, since they result from the splitting of a single zygote after conception. Fraternal (non-identical) twins, on the other hand, have only 50 percent common heredity because they result from the separate fertilization of two eggs by two sperm—just like ordinary brothers and sisters. It follows that if the genes are important determinants of the trait in question, identical twins will be more alike than fraternal twins.

Using such a technique, it has been shown that homosexual orientation is to some extent predisposed by heredity and that a person's level of libido is also strongly influenced by genetic factors (see Eysenck and Wilson, 1979). While it is too early to assign exact proportions to the roles of heredity and environment in these areas, the early indications are that around a half to two-thirds of the variation in sex orientation (homo versus hetero) and libido (strong versus weak sexual drive) may turn out to be determined by the genes. Heredity also seems to play a part in sexual satisfaction—but perhaps not so much as the other aspects of sexuality. Of course, this percentage also depends upon the prevailing social conditions; the move toward greater tolerance and permissiveness that we are witnessing today is probably increasing the extent to which sexual behavior is genetically determined. If all social pressure is removed and learning experiences are equalized by mass-media presentation and standardized education, most of the differences in behavior between one person and another will be of "natural" origin.

When it comes to the particular variations with which this book is concerned, no really useful evidence is available concerning the role of genetic factors. One or two case studies have been reported in which remarkably similar fetishist or tranvestite behavior has been observed in identical twins. In a case reported by Gorman in 1964, for example, a rubber fetishism had apparently developed independently in a pair of identical twins. Neither knew of the other's predilection until the age of ten even though their interest in rubber had begun at the ages of five and six respectively. When in adulthood one of them sought medical advice at the instigation of his wife, the two twins related remarkably similar histories with similar (though not coincident) formative incidents.

Case studies of this kind are interesting because they indicate the possibility of genetic involvement, but of course they are "uncontrolled" in the sense that the evidence tends to be selective. No doubt it would be easy to find cases of identical twins who did not share a similar interest in fetishism. This is why a larger twin study is called for to assess the extent to which such predilections are inherited. A beginning has been made by Wilson to assemble enough twin data to answer this question, but unfortunately, this looks to be a lengthy process and the study is far from complete. It involved asking pairs of identical and fraternal twins to complete the Sex Fantasy Questionnaire and to return it anonymously with a code number to the researcher so that the twin pairs could later be linked up. Table 10 shows some preliminary data from this continuing study. Although the sample of fourteen male pairs of each type of twin is too small to give a stable indication of the relative importance of genes and environment, it is presented here because it remains the best evidence available so far.

In Table 10 we have picked out three key themes from the Fantasy Questionnaire: sadomasochism, fetishism and transvestism respectively. These have been scored for each subject by adding up the five columns in the questionnaire,

Table 10. Intraclass correlations of identical and fraternal twins on key fantasy items, self-rated sex drive and overall sexual satisfaction.
(These correlations are based on fourteen pairs of identical twins and fourteen pairs of fraternal twins, all male.)

	Identical twins	Fraternal twins
Being whipped or spanked	0.36	0.13
Being excited by material or clothing	0.37	0.50
Wearing clothes of the opposite sex	0.80	0.43
Sex drive	0.42	0.02
Satisfaction	0.52	0.17

thus combining fantasy and reality ratings of various kinds to give an overall index of interest in the theme. In order to replicate the earlier work on the genetics of sexuality by Eysenck (1976) we have also included libido and satisfaction in this preliminary analysis. Product-moment correlations were calculated for each type of twin on each measure of sexual style.

Although with only fourteen pairs of twins for each correlation very few of them attain statistical significance, there is an apparent tendency for the identical twins to be more alike than the fraternal twins. This is particularly true of satisfaction, libido and transvestism; it is less obvious with respect to sadomasochism, and the fetishistic item actually shows a slight difference in the wrong direction. While we should be careful not to over-interpret results based on such small numbers, they do adhere very well to theoretical expectation. Of our three main sexual variations, fetishism is the one that theorists have most often pointed to as fitting a conditioning model. For example, Rachman and Hodgson (1976), in a now famous conditioning study, showed that it was possible to create in the laboratory an experimental boot fetish by taking a group of men with no particular interest in boots and having them associate boot pictures with pictures of nude women. Moreover, they were able to show that the association process followed the laws of classical conditioning established in Pavlov's famous studies of canine salivation, in that the boot pictures had to *precede* those of nude women. Conditioning did not occur when pictures of boots *followed* those of nude women. Studies such as this suggest that learning factors are likely to be involved in the development of fetishes, so it is perhaps not so surprising that our twin study so far shows no evidence of heredity in fetishism.

Sadomasochism seems to yield a genetic factor in this study rather like those emerging for sex drive and satisfaction, and the Eysenck results show every likelihood of being supported by the present study. But if the present trend is sustained, the results for the transvestism theme may turn out to be the most interesting of all. A genetic factor is indicated by the fact that the correlation for the identical twins is considerably higher than that for the fraternal twins, but the fact that *both* correlations are quite high suggests that family learning experiences are also implicated in the urge to cross-dress. These family influences make for considerable similarity in the behavior of the fraternal twins, despite their genetic differences, while the combined effects of heredity and environment make for an even higher degree of correlation between the identical twins.

Although these results should be taken as preliminary only, they hint toward the conclusion that fetishisms are largely learned (inside and outside of the home), that sadomasochism is influenced by genetic factors and random (i.e. nonfamily) learning experiences and that transvestism is derived from the family, both genetically and environmentally. It will be interesting to see to what extent these hypotheses are borne out at the conclusion of our study and by future research.

One point needs clarifying before we proceed to our findings concerning the effects of upbringing and other learning experiences. The twin study above will at best group causes broadly into those that are genetic and those that are environmental. Given sufficient numbers it may also be possible to assess the relative importance of the family environment against other, nonfamily environmental influences. But what is often forgotten is that environmental effects include physical influences as well as social. When we talk about the "environmental component," we do not only refer to the way in which people are treated by parents, relatives, teachers and other significant people. We also include the effects of diseases like meningitis, brain injury at birth or in a later accident and prenatal influences, such as drugs taken by the mother during pregnancy. Thus, there are many biological determinants, other than genetic, to sexual behavior, and these are treated as environmental within the logic of twin studies.

Just how important these nongenetic biological effects are, in connection with sexual variations of the kind we have been studying, is difficult to say at the moment. There is a suggestion that fetishism and transvestism may sometimes be linked with minor damage to the temporal lobe of the brain, of the kind that also sometimes causes epilepsy (Epstein, 1961). But this is most unlikely to account for all cases of such variation. Damage to the brain can cause any kind of behavior or symptom, depending upon where in the brain the damage occurs, but this does not prove it is the normal origin of that behavior. For example, the pioneering studies of brain surgeon Wilder Penfield showed that electrical stimulation of the surface of the temporal lobe would in some patients evoke a childhood memory or a musical experience, but this is not the way we usually remember things or listen to one of Beethoven's symphonies. Still, the possibility remains open that some cases of fetishism, transvestism and other unusual sexual behaviors, especially those which seem very compulsive and ego-alien to the individual concerned, can properly be considered to have resulted from subtle brain lesions.

Another important research program which seems to have relevance to constitutional factors in human sexuality is that conducted by John Money and associates at Johns Hopkins Hospital in Baltimore. This work has revealed that the treatment of a mother with progesterone-like hormones towards the end of her pregnancy—a treatment sometimes carried out in the 1950s to reduce the chances of a miscarriage—could alter the orientation of female children to make them more masculine in their interests and behavior, though not necessarily lesbian. Other work by Money suggests that there is a critical period for gender identification after which it is almost impossible successfully to change the self-concept. If surgery designed to give a child genitals that are consistent with his or her chromosomal sex is carried out before the age of two, then that child will be able to switch gender identity without much trouble. After this age, however, the child is so likely to experience difficulties that it is usually better to reinforce his or her identity as "boy" or "girl" regardless of the chromosomes.

Work such as this suggests the importance of both constitutional and early learning experiences as well as genetic influences, and the untangling of these effects is unlikely to be accomplished in the near future. We can, however, infer that constitutional factors are of particular importance in transvestism and transsexualism, as well as in other general orientations such as homosexuality, while learning experiences play a more significant role in determining the sexual cues and signals that we will eventually use in adult life. Probably there are certain people who, by dint of constitution or temperament, are particularly likely to develop a fetishistic attachment to some object or material. No doubt there are also certain qualities in materials such as rubber, leather, silk and fur that make them particularly suited to being targets of such attachments. But which material selected by a given individual is much more likely to be determined by learning experiences? And what sort of learning experiences are they?

In a way, it is surprising that the Rachman and Hodgson experiment was so successful, because it was conducted on adult males who had presumably already established their own set of sexual connections. This is just as well if the conditioning model is to lend itself to treatment, i.e. rearrangement of the learned connections. Clinical experience, however, would lead us to suggest that, at least as regards the origins of sexual preferences, the relevant learning would take place earlier in life, perhaps at certain critical periods of development, and would involve relationships with and feelings about other people and high degrees of arousal.

Let us examine the process in action by considering just one case history. In it we will notice that the adult sexual pattern bears at least some resemblance to the childhood experiences described. Nevertheless, it would probably be a mistake to regard these memories as either a single traumatic experience, or even necessarily exactly true. What does come through far more strongly when one talks to people like Mr. C. in the

following case history, is that their childhoods contained people whose attitudes, over a considerable period, are symbol-
ized in the experience or experiences related. What seems in
a childhood memory to be a single "learning" experience may
well be a multiplicity of learning experiences which in time
created the beginnings of the adult fantasy in a slightly different and probably more manageable guise.

Mr. C. is now sixty years old, but looks younger. He was born to
upper-middle-class parents, and his birth was normal. His mother
died one year later from influenza. The relationship between his
parents was reported as having been good, though not close because his father spent many years of his life working away from
home. Like his two older brothers and older sister, Mr. C. spent
his early years with his grandmother and an aunt, and later with a
female guardian. All belonged to the professional classes. Mr. C.
was a "late developer" academically. He went to boarding school,
where he had "some bad times—but then everyone did in those
days. Mine were largely due to being slow to learn." He mixed
well, was not bullied and did well at sports. Mr. C. has few memories of home life with his grandmother and aunt, but was on good
terms with his brothers and sister, especially with his next older
brother. He did, however, form a close, eventually homosexual
relationship with the family chauffeur. He has a particularly strong
memory of himself, at age nine, fellating this chauffeur, who was
wearing a rubberized raincoat and high boots.

At the age of twelve he went to live with a female guardian. This
woman clearly had a strong effect on him; the fact that she was a
firm disciplinarian may not have been unexceptional in the 1920s
but his calm assertion that "she enjoyed whipping me" is supported by his claim that she often did so, yet did not always attempt
to use much force. When pressed as to whether an actual whip was
used, he replied, "Well, sometimes a cane, but mostly a riding
whip." During one of these punishments, he accidentally uri-
nated; on subsequent occasions he was laid on a rubber sheet or a
mackintosh before being punished and he remembers experienc-
ing orgasm under these conditions on more than one occasion.

In terms of more conventional sex education, Mr. C. states that
he learned "the elementary details" in primary school, but that he
never attempted to expand that knowledge, preferring his developing masochistic fantasies. He did not begin to masturbate until
he was fifteen. During his later developmental years, he also acquired a fetishistic attraction for velvet, which his guardian, but

not his grandmother or aunt, very often wore. His early attitude toward masturbation was guilt; his feeling toward his homosexual behavior was that he "didn't like it at first, but grew to accept it later."

Because of his late academic development, he started work in the diplomatic service at the age of twenty-three, having first acquired an honors degree at Oxford. He married after a three-year courtship, and had a daughter and a son, though the latter died in infancy. His relationship with his wife was good, but she did not cooperate in realizing his particular fantasies. "Mind you, I didn't force the issue with her," he says. "She has her own problems. Nevertheless, I had a lot of time for her, as a person." They were, however, eventually divorced. Mr. C. has since visited prostitutes, preferring black women in spite of the fact that they seldom played out his ritualized fantasies to his liking and, according to him, seldom even understood his requirements. He also mentioned a homosexual relationship with a young black boy.

Mr. C.'s present behavior is somewhat influenced by the fact that he has recently formed a relationship with a woman to whom he clearly wishes to present himself as being behaviorally free from the fantasies which he describes. His manner is friendly and relaxed, and he converses easily. One might suspect that, because Mr. C.'s memories fit not only the pattern of many pornographic inventions but also his own present favorite fantasies, he inadvertently may have post-fabricated them. Mr. C. denies this strongly, however, and we are prepared to accept at least that *he* believes these memories to be largely accurate and that his fantasies are truthfully set out. His fantasies center, as might be expected, around "interrogation" episodes involving whipping while confined in rubber.

"I suppose that my favorite fantasy, out of about ten, is that I am at a boarding school, aged about ten, and have been caught having sexual relations with another boy. I have been confined to the hospital pending removal by my aunt and grandmother, my father being abroad. My relatives seek the aid of my rich godmother, known to me as arrogant and puritanical. They arrive in a Daimler car, and while grandmother and aunt interview the matron and the headmaster, my godmother's robust, half-caste maids (dressed in boots, mackintoshes and breeches and looking like uniformed chauffers) come to take me away. I resist them, kicking out wildly, but am eventually overpowered and am taken on a lead, with a rubber cape tied over my head, to the car, bound tightly and shoved on the floor, the boots of the maids holding me still as they sit on the back seat.

"After interrogation and confession as described above, I am sentenced to one hundred strokes carried out over ten days. The method of whipping is important: it is done cold-bloodedly and ritualistically, with plenty of time between strokes—time during which I have to repeat an episode revealed in my confession-story. I am tied over a rubber-covered high hassock, so that writhings induce an orgasm. When this is discovered, I receive more strokes. These strokes are always delivered precisely and aimed accurately with a thin cane, a plaited leather whip or rubber hose, or an old-fashioned birch dipped in salt water or vinegar. At the end of each session, balm or ointment is rubbed onto my burning buttocks, and this makes me want to masturbate again, but my hands remain tied.

"My confessions of course implicate other boys and staff, including the matron, so they get invited by my godmother to the house for questioning—but that is another story."

Clearly, many of the episodes mentioned in Mr. C.'s history come up again in the fantasy described. One is reminded strongly of Robert Stoller's (1976) view of the function of sexual fantasy: "Sexual excitement," he writes, "depends on a scenario that the person to be aroused has been writing since childhood. The story is an adventure, an autobiography disguised as fiction, in which the hero/heroine hides crucial intrapsychic conflicts, mysteries, screen memories of actual traumatic events and the resolution of these elements into a happy ending, best celebrated by orgasm. The function of the fantasy is to take these painful elements and convert them to pleasure—triumph. In order to sharpen excitement—the vibration between the fear of original traumas repeating and the hope of a pleasurable conclusion this time—one introduces into the story elements of risk (approximations to the original trauma) meant to prevent boredom, and safety factors (subliminal signals to the story teller that the risks are not truly dangerous)." Such an interpretation allows us to see why, even if it does not much help us to predict when, some fantasists attempt to convert their fantasies into reality by acting them out, while others do not. To the latter, even the possibility that trauma will overcome triumph produces enough anxiety to prevent them from acting out the fantasy even under controlled circumstances, such as the prostitute's "playroom" or the understanding partner's cooperation.

THE ROLE OF PUNISHMENT IN CHILDHOOD

The problem with case-history analyses and clinical interpretations such as Stoller's is that it is often difficult to see how they can be proved right or wrong. Yet if Mr. C.'s experience of punishment was an important determinant of his sadomasochistic predilection then we might predict that sadomasochists as a group would recall a greater incidence of corporal punishment in childhood than men who did not show this predilection. The data shown in Table 11 do not bear out this hypothesis. Our sadomasochists report slightly more beatings in childhood than control males but this difference is so small as to be insignificant. Nor do the rubberites, leatherites or transvestites have an excessive experience of punishment. As a matter of fact, the leatherites actually report less corporal punishment in childhood than the controls, though again the difference is too small to be counted as reliable.

Even when experience of punishment is investigated separately in relation to the different types of fantasy within each of the variant and control groups, the role of punishment

Table 11. Mean scores (and standard deviations) of variant and control groups on certain aspects of social background and upbringing. (For exact questions and response format see Sex Fantasy Questionaire in Chapter 2.)

	Sado-masochists	Rubber-ites	Leather-ites	Transvest-ites	Controls
Percentage with partner	57	69	66	64	78
Permissiveness of upbringing	2.04(1.1)	2.04(.9)	2.00(.8)	2.01(.9)	2.30(1.1)
Freedom from inhibition	3.40(1.4)	3.11(1.3)	3.74(1.1)	2.98(1.2)	3.44(1.1)
Experience of corporal punishment	2.73(1.1)	2.70(.7)	2.32(.9)	2.66(1.2)	2.68(1.0)

seems to be minimal. The only significant finding is that rubberites who report a great deal of punishment are more likely to have masochistic fantasies (interestingly, the very association that seems to have occurred in the case of Mr. C.). Still, this is a fairly small correlation and will need verification by later research.

These results must come as a disappointment to people who believe that corporal punishment inflicted on young people has such heavy sexual undertones that the recipient is almost bound to grow up with overheated fantasies of sexual "punishment." On the other hand, we cannot say that our findings rule out the possibility that punishment is an important precipitating factor in sadomasochism. Aspects of the punishment, other than its frequency, might be crucial: the manner in which the punishment was delivered; the relationship with the administrator; the pain inflicted; whether or not it was deserved. It is complications like these that prompt some clinicians to argue that scientific generalizations are of no use because every individual is unique.

PERMISSIVENESS OF UPBRINGING

One of the most consistent findings to come out of research on sexual deviation is that people who develop unusual sexual patterns are likely to have had a more restrictive than average upbringing. This trend is detectable in Table 12, in which all

Table 12. Correlations between incidence of corporal punishment in childhood and various types of sexual fantasy for variant and control groups.

	Type of fantasy		
	Intimate	Sadistic	Masochistic
Sadomasochists	—0.05	0.09	0.14
Rubberites	0.04	0.05	0.23
Leatherites	0.09	0.14	0.04
Transvestites	0.11	0.02	0.08
Controls	0.03	—0.05	—0.04

the variant groups appear at least to have perceived their own upbringing as fairly strict by comparison with the controls. However, these differences are very small and do not reach statistical significance.

Response to the question about how inhibited subjects considered themselves shows a rather different pattern in Table 12. The transvestites regard themselves as more inhibited than the controls, presumably because they feel their freedom to express themselves by wearing female clothes—in public at least—is limited. The leatherites, on the other hand, claim to be relatively free of inhibition; a claim consistent with certain indications in the previous chapter that this group tends to be rather rebellious in personality.

PRESENCE OR ABSENCE OF PARTNER

Table 12 also shows that the percentage of people in each of the variant groups having a steady partner is lower than that of the control group. This could be interpreted as meaning that variants have problems developing and maintaining steady relationships. Alternatively, one could claim that the variant either does not want a steady partner (because this would interfere with his variant activities) or does not need a partner (because his variant activities are enough to remove any frustration he might have). Yet another interpretation might be that the lack of a partner encourages the maintenance of variant behavior. We have in this instance no particular preference for any one of these hypotheses, but this illustration shows how easily speculation in this field can outrun knowledge.

AGE DISTRIBUTION

Examination of the ages of the members of our variant groups (Figure 6) shows a surprising similarity in the average age, namely, between forty-one and forty-four years old. The distribution, however, is slightly askew, with the most frequently occurring ages in the forty-five to forty-nine range.

Is this figure significant in terms of there having been a particularly stressful or fruitful time during which many of our subjects were developing sexually, giving rise to a greater incidence of, or predisposition to, variant behavior? This is the type of explanation favored by those who believe in the

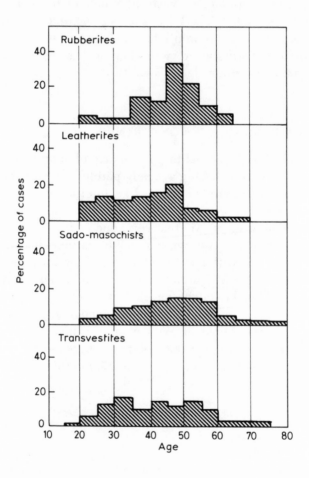

Figure 6. Age distributions of the four main groups of male variants.

power of the environment to shape our destiny. On the other hand, it may be argued that as the male gets older, the excitement of conventional sex palls and leads him to try other modes of expression to obtain sexual satisfaction. Another age-distribution theory would be that individuals with variant sexual interests are being "continuously created" at an equal rate, but the younger element has not felt the need or desire to join a group in order to further the expression of that interest. In the absence of further evidence this would seem to be the simplest way of accounting for the age structure of our groups.

Closer examination of the age distribution for each group, however, does reveal some interesting differences. Whereas the two fetishistic groups and the sadomasochistic group exhibit a single peak in the forty-five to forty-nine range, the transvestite group has an additional peak in the thirty to thirty-four range. This is consistent with the idea that this group contains two types of transvestite, the fetishistic individual and the "true" or gender-orienting type, whose learning curves begin at different ages or proceed at different speeds. Presumably the older group contains more of the fetishistic type and the younger group more of the "true" transvestites.

In the case of the rubber fetishistic group, we can offer a suggestion as to the nature of the "stressful period" which might have been partly responsible for the variant behavior. In some earlier work by Gosselin (1979) with the same group of fetishists, it was found that the majority of rubberites were first aroused by rubber between the ages of four and ten (Figure 7). Combining this information with the typical ages of Mackintosh Society members in 1978 (forty-five to fifty), we can derive that the most likely time in which our rubber fetishistic group acquired their attraction for the material was around the beginning of the Second World War in 1939. It is easy to understand how this period in England might be considered particularly appropriate for the development of such a predilection—the early war years were especially anxiety-provoking times, with absent fathers, consequently over-protective mothers, family separations due to death or evacuation to the country to avoid bombing raids, plus relevant stimuli, such as the gas mask which attracts so many rubberites, raincapes, groundsheets and so on. Not to be overlooked are the slightly more removed symbolic associations that connect certain sadomasochistic fantasies with the Nazi image of jackboots, rubber raincoats and riding crops. We leave it to the reader, however, to judge to what extent this "stress period" is coincidental; we are not in any case trying to argue that every fetishist developed his liking because of that particular set of associations. On the other hand, it does raise the possibility that national as well as personal traumas can cause such developments.

One more interesting finding emerges from our age data. During the period in which we were getting to know our subjects, one fetishist remarked, "People should envy us rather than back off from us: we've got a stone-cold, guaranteed aphrodisiac that can turn us on at any time, however old we are."

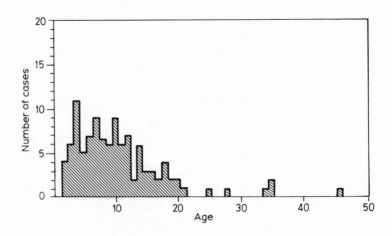

Figure 7. The ages at which one hundred rubber fetishists first recognized their attraction to rubber.

Later on, in the magazine issued by the sadomasochistic society whose members formed our group, a lady member wrote, "I have learned . . . that masochistic desire in a man usually gets stronger and more insistent as age advances." This remark was followed with the idea that since it is well known that the frequency of intercourse decreases with age, the cooperative woman can improve her sex life with a maslochistically inclined man by the inclusion of a suitable dominant-submissive play-game. Investigation of the correlations between age and the frequency of specific appropriate fantasies showed that both these statements have some truth to them, even if both contain an element of wishful thinking. While it cannot be said that any particular variant fantasy increases in intensity with age, it appears that the fantasy appropriate to the variant group decreases at a slower rate than does the base-line fantasy of "intercourse with a loved partner." The reverse is true for males of the control group, in that fantasies concerning intercourse with a loved one decrease with age more slowly than do any variant fantasies the group might have. Such a trend within a partnership where one member enjoys variant activities and the other goes along with them is therefore something of a two-edged sword for the couple. Although it could be utilized by them—as it apparently was in the case of the lady writing in the sadomasochist's magazine—as a means by which sexual interaction can be prolonged and intensified with the use of a suitable play-game, there is a danger that their diverging favorite themes may become a bone of contention between them as they get older.

OCCUPATIONAL STATUS

We end this examination of the social background of our subjects with a brief glance at their social-class status. This is of interest because there is conflicting folklore on the matter. Some people find it impossible to conceive that grown men can behave in the ways described for our variant groups, without being intellectually as well as emotionally immature. If this were the case, the members of our variant groups would have difficulty holding down responsible jobs and would drift toward lower-class occupations. A counter view, promulgated particularly by tabloid newspapers, is that of a corrupt aristocracy practicing all kinds of kinky sex in response either to boredom or boarding-school discipline, because they have the power, money and leisure to indulge themselves. As one prostitute told us, "The man in the street likes blonde curls and bright red lipstick, the middle-class man wants black stockings and a look up your skirt before he starts, but the upper-class man goes for fladge [flagellation], tying up and the rest of it." The attitude of the general public toward this imagined perversion of the nobility is somewhere between disdain for an upper class that has lost its way and fallen into decadence, and envy of a group who are suspected to be connoisseurs of sexuality as much as food and wine. Are either of these viewpoints supported by a social-class analysis of our variant groups?

In our study, occupations were rated on a five-point scale. Broadly speaking, higher professional and businesspersons such as doctors, lawyers and corporate directors are classed as Group 1, lower professionals and businesspersons like teachers, civil administrators and owners of small businesses are rated 2, clerks and other "white collar" workers are classed as 3, tradesmen and skilled workers 4, and unskilled workers, such as laborers and cleaners, 5. Thus in Table 13, a lower-than-average occupational level implies a higher social class in the group. However, the variant groups are hardly distinguishable from each other and their average—between classes 2 and 3—places them slightly higher in occupational status than the median of the British population, though slightly lower than our controls. This is hardly sufficient to support the idea that they represent an upper-class underground, and the variance (represented by the standard deviation in Table 13) is about what one would expect of a group

Table 13.   Average socio-economic status of variant and control groups.
(The scale runs from 1=higher professional and business to 5=unskilled worker.)

Group	Mean occupational status (and standard deviation)
Sadomasochists	2.72(1.0)
Rubberites	2.38(1.0)
Leatherites	2.45(0.9)
Transvestites	2.75(1.1)
Transsexuals	3.00(0.7)
Dominant women	2.56(0.7)
Male controls	2.14(0.9)
Female controls	2.56(0.6)

drawn fairly randomly from the population. In other words, there is no indication of bimodality, such as would occur if the groups were comprised of upper- *and* lower-class members with relatively few middle-class people.

This finding needs no psychological comment, except perhaps to point out that the woman who caters professionally to variants may be of the opinion that they are above average in social status because only the comparatively affluent can afford to visit such women in the first place. Such an idea of "selection by wealth" may also explain why the fetishists seem of marginally higher average socio-economic level than the transvestite or the sadomasochist. Fetishistic costumes are often extremely complex and are sometimes custom-made. As a result, their cost is high, provoking the comment from a less affluent member at a Mackintosh Society meeting, "To be a proper fetishist, you've got to be loaded."

7

Transsexuals and Mistresses

At almost any moment in a research worker's professional life, there is a certain amount of "unfinished business"—preliminary studies, partial data assemblies, information on minorities within minorities and so on. Whether such material should be included in a published work depends to a great extent on the ease with which a larger, better, more complete study could be performed. If data is hard to come by, then half a loaf may be better than no bread, even in scientific circles.

It is for this reason that we have included in this chapter such data as we have on two small groups of sexually different people, namely, male-to-female transsexuals and those whom we will for the moment describe as sexually adventurous women. The first group contains only sixteen members, all belonging to the Beaumont Society from which the transvestite data was obtained, but the information that these sixteen supplied shows sufficient differences from the transvestites and the control group to be of interest. The second group consists of twenty-five women who either belonged to the society for sadomasochists from which our male sample was drawn, or who had placed advertisements in an independent contact magazine aimed at those with sadomasochistic tendencies. Our object was directly to compare men and women with sadomasochistic tendencies. We may in fact have done this, but as will be seen later, the women in question turned out to be more than just sadomasochists.

Incidentally, the latter group is not "artificial" in the sense that it comprises women who are merely putting on an act for the benefit of their partners. There were several safeguards against this happening. We had assurance from the society of the genuineness of their members and we had at least the pragmatic opinion from the contact magazine, *Superbitch*, that those advertisers who were not genuine would never bother to send in data. Also, our questionnaire contained items concerning the extent to which the respondent's sadomasochistic activities were for her own enjoyment rather than merely put on for her partner's sake, and the extent to which her activities were linked to material—or financial—reward. Evidence both from our questionnaire and from follow-up interviews indicates that members of this group are likely to have been just as honest in their replies as the other groups with which we have been dealing.

For the moment, however, let us return to our transsexual group. Examination of replies to the Wilson questionnaire shows first that, as Benjamin would have predicted, we are dealing with a group whose libido is very low. This is seen in Table 14 in terms of their total fantasy output, which is about half that of the male control group, or the transvestites for that matter, and in the various indices of sex drive shown in Table 15. This generally low level of libido naturally affects the theme-by-theme comparisons between them and their control counterparts. The results show significantly lower fantasy levels concerning sex with a known, untried partner, sex with an anonymous partner, sex with two other people, participating in an orgy, forcing and being forced sexually, giving and receiving oral sex, watching others have sex, taking someone's clothes off, making love elsewhere than in the bedroom, having sex with someone much younger, having sex with some-

Table 14. Fantasy ratings for transsexual and "superbitch" groups compared with male and female control groups.

	Transsexuals	Control Males	Dominant Women	Control Females
1. Making love out of doors in a romantic setting (e.g. field of flowers, beach at night).	0.78	1.23	1.58	1.06
2. Having intercourse with a loved partner.	1.31	1.95	2.70	2.98
3. Intercourse with someone you know but have not had sex with.	0.78	2.13	1.90	2.17
4. Intercourse with an anonymous stranger.	0.13	1.33	1.88	1.0
5. Sex with two other people.	0.09	1.10	1.84	0.81
6. Participating in an orgy.	0.19	0.86	1.56	0.09
7. Being forced to do something.	0.56	0.19	1.46	1.00
8. Forcing someone to do something.	0.00	0.56	2.06	0.60
9. Homosexual activity.	0.63	0.47	1.14	0.54
10. Receiving oral sex.	0.56	1.85	2.58	1.73
11. Giving oral sex.	0.78	1.82	2.26	1.60
12. Watching others have sex.	0.22	1.10	1.42	0.83
13. Sex with an animal.	0.00	0.04	0.48	0.08
14. Whipping or spanking someone.	0.06	0.29	1.92	0.15
15. Being whipped or spanked.	0.13	0.11	1.42	0.23

16. Taking someone's clothes off.	0.44	1.84	1.34	1.60
17. Having your clothes taken off.	1.03	1.33	2.10	1.77
18. Making love elsewhere than in the bedroom (e.g. kitchen, bathroom).	0.34	1.49	2.34	2.00
19. Being excited by material or clothing (e.g. rubber, leather, underwear).	1.03	0.80	1.64	0.25
20. Hurting a partner.	0.00	0.17	1.38	0.46
21. Being hurt by a partner.	0.18	0.10	1.17	0.40
22. Mate-swapping	0.22	0.77	1.37	0.42
23. Being aroused by watching someone urinate.	0.00	0.13	0.99	0.17
24. Being tied up.	0.13	0.18	1.39	0.50
25. Tying someone up.	0.03	0.46	1.84	0.27
26. Having incestuous sexual relations.	0.00	0.10	0.95	0.17
27. Exposing yourself provocatively.	0.22	0.18	1.71	0.92
28. Transvestism (wearing clothes of the opposite sex).	2.14	0.12	0.98	0.00
29. Being promiscuous.	0.41	1.08	1.74	1.06
30. Having sex with someone much younger than yourself.	0.25	1.46	1.78	0.69
31. Having sex with someone much older than yourself.	0.53	1.16	1.58	0.42
32. Being much sought after by the opposite sex.	0.50	1.21	1.84	1.75

(Continued)

(Continued)

	Transsexuals	Control Males	Dominant Women	Control Females
33. Being seduced as an "innocent."	0.41	0.48	1.72	0.63
34. Seducing an "innocent."	0.19	0.92	1.65	0.54
35. Being embarrassed by failure of sexual performance.	0.16	0.36	1.03	0.19
36. Having sex with someone of different race.	0.13	0.94	1.26	0.60
37. Using objects for stimulation. (e.g. vibrators, candles).	0.63	0.64	1.54	0.52
38. Being masturbated to orgasm by a partner.	0.81	1.63	1.80	1.69
39. Looking at obscene pictures or films.	0.25	1.10	1.66	0.75
40. Kissing passionately.	1.63	1.68	1.87	2.10
Mean (over items)	0.45	0.87	1.62	0.87

Table 15.   Comparison of transsexuals, dominant women and control groups on various aspects of sex life and upbringing.
(Most of the figures are mean ratings on a 1–5 scale.)

	Transsexuals	Control males	Dominant women	Control females
With steady partner	25%	78%	67%	83%
Sexual satisfaction with partner	2.75	3.38	4.12	3.35
Overall satisfaction	1.94	3.02	3.52	3.33
Orgasms per week	1.50	2.46	3.08	2.63
Self-rated sex drive	1.87	3.20	3.88	3.62
No. of partners	1.94	3.56	3.80	3.04
Permissiveness of upbringing	2.25	2.30	2.24	2.29
Freedom from inhibition	2.31	3.44	3.60	3.50
Experience of corporal punishment	2.50	2.68	2.52	2.70

one of a different race and looking at obscene pictures or films. Only the criterion of wearing clothes of the opposite sex elicited, quite naturally, a far higher incidence among transsexuals than among the controls.

In order to round out the picture that the transsexual presents to the world we must look positively at such fantasies as do occur in this group. It seems that the male-to-female transsexual displays, although at quite a low level, a very conventional or intimate set of fantasies, similar in fact to those which previous research has shown are typical of normal women. The transsexual's favorite fantasies (excluding those of being dressed as a woman—for they are the natural accompaniment of all the other fantasies) are of kissing, having intercourse with a loved partner, being undressed, being masturbated to orgasm by a partner, having sex with a known but untried partner, giving—but not receiving—oral sex and being excited by materials or clothing; his or her actual experience also reflects that pattern.

But while she may have achieved her goal of being a woman in terms of fantasy, activity and way of life, it cannot be said that the transsexual person's sexual situation is entirely desirable by conventional standards. She has only a 25 percent chance of having a steady partner (as against a 65 percent chance for the transvestite and a 78 percent chance for the control group member), and her satisfaction with her partner, if any, is on average lower than that of any other group. Her satisfaction with her general sex life is well below average, as is the number of orgasms she has per week. She has had intercourse with a smaller number of partners than average, and although she does not consider her upbringing to have been more restrictive than that of either the control group or her transvestite co-members of the Beaumont Society, she rates herself as rather more sexually inhibited than either of these groups. If anything, she appears to have received slightly less corporal punishment at school than other comparable groups. We have also seen in the previous chapter that the transsexual is particularly prone to loneliness and despair.

This situation has of course long been known at an experiential level by both clinical workers and the transsexual herself. Unlike the other types of variant studied in this book, transsexuals must have attended a clinic, unless they class themselves as transsexual as a result of merely having lived as a woman for some time without detection. The clinician has thus learned a lot about the transsexual, and is well aware of the difficulties to be overcome and the burden to be borne by her. Some specialists, indeed, have come to the conclusion that those burdens are too much for anyone to take on. In his book *Sex Change* (1970), Gilbert Oakley writes, "From my observations, I am convinced that the transvestite is far happier than the transsexual. Life is by no means so complex, so painful or so embarrassing for him. The future is not obscured by a mist of hopefulness and doubt. The best of two worlds lies within the transvestite's grasp, for he can change from male to 'female' at will." This author concludes that the sex-change phenomenon is wholly and completely disastrous, and that "medical bodies the world over are seriously at fault in encouraging it in any way when other means of therapy are surely at their disposal to help these unfortunate people."

Such a view, we nevertheless believe, is rather unjust.

Other means of therapy may be available, but it cannot be said that any of them are very effective, and in any case the transsexual has not the slightest wish to avail himself of them. His wish is simply to be a woman, and he rejects any other alternative. There is also the danger of forming an opinion based on observing transsexuals who are conspicuous because of their maladjustment. In any one year, many people throughout the world change their sex; the majority are male-to-female transsexuals who slip quietly away to make a life in which their success as a woman is evident from the fact that nobody ever questions their state.

Yet, whatever his view on the advisability of the sex-change operation, the clinician will have no doubts about the intense desire which motivates the transsexual to move from one sex to the other. He will also have noticed the very early age (compared to that of the transvestite) at which the wish to be womanly is manifested. He will see nothing new in our finding that, in spite of a significant similarity between both the fantasies and the past activities of the transvestite and the transsexual (the correlations being 0.84 and 0.88 respectively), the transvestite cross-dresses more for sexual excitement than does the transsexual, who cross-dresses mainly because he feels himself to be a woman.

An original piece of data contributing to the controversy over the differentiation between the transvestite and the transsexual comes from the measure of fetishistic behavior in transsexuals. Stoller (1971) has argued that fetishism cannot occur in this group because erotic pleasure for the transsexual is not centered in the penis. Two Australian psychiatrists, Buhrich and McConaghy (1977), however, reported signs of fetishistic arousal to women's clothes in five out of twenty-nine transsexuals whom they studied. Our results show that, while fetishistic behavior and fantasy do occur in our transsexuals, they do not occur to any great extent—in fact not significantly more so than in our controls.

The question is an interesting one, because if fetishism was reliably present in the transvestite but not in the transsexual then this phenomenon could be used as a diagnostic test to distinguish one from the other. However, several members of our transvestite group show very low ratings on the question about excitement due to materials or clothing and deny that they cross-dress in order to obtain sexual arousal, claiming that they do so because they feel that they belong (or wish to belong) to the opposite sex. It is therefore clear that the presence or absence of fetishistic fantasy or behavior would not reliably distinguish the transvestite from the transsexual. In fact, we may speculate as to whether Benjamin's "true" (i.e. nonfetishistic) transvestite is not closer to being a transsexual in all but estrogen and operation than he ever dreamed he was. One can sense this betwixt-and-between status in the transvestite's fantasy of wishing to be made love to by a man while disclaiming homosexual feelings; Oakley clarifies this by pointing out that while the homosexual may want his ideal partner to be homosexual as well, the true transvestite will want that partner to be a normal heterosexual male.

The personality scores of the transsexual group given in Table 5, Chapter 5, show them to be fairly similar to transvestites on extraversion, neuroticism and psychoticism. Both groups are rather introverted compared with normal males and females; in fact, they are the most introverted of all the variant groups. In terms of the neuroticism dimension, they are higher in emotionality than normal males but only slightly higher than female controls. Their psychoticism scores are more in the range of the control males than the control females, but it would be difficult to interpret this without looking in more detail at the particular items which they endorse. It will be remembered from Chapter 6, for example, that transsexuals are certainly not characterized by dislike of their mothers. In any case, the transsexual does not display personality characteristics that would lead one to classify her in any way with clinical neurotics or psychotics. The slightly elevated lie-scale score of the transsexuals relative to all the other groups suggests, rather paradoxically perhaps, that they are in certain respects conforming and concerned about giving a good impression. It is most unlikely under the circumstances that they are making any outright attempt to deceive the researchers.

If we compare the transsexual's personality profile, as well as her scores on all the other variables we have studied, with those of the male and female control data, we can see that she resembles a woman at least as much if not more than she does a male. The interesting point about this is that over the years an impressive amount of evidence has been produced to support the idea that personality variables in particular are very little subject to environmental influence. Rather, their level is largely biologically "set" and they have a remarkable degree of stability (Wilson, 1976). It is therefore quite likely that the male-to-female transsexual is womanly not merely because she lives as a woman or because she has had surgical treatment to match her physical attributes with her self-concept, but that her personality was womanly before the particular way of life developed and/or the surgery complemented it. Of course, we would need to produce longitudinal evidence to properly support this idea, particularly personality testing before any hormone treatment had been given (or self-administered), but still it remains a very plausible hypothesis.

So much then for a group of males that have moved in all senses toward being female. Let us now examine a group of females who, without losing any of their femininity, have assumed at least some of the sexual role assumed traditionally by men.

SEXUALLY ADVENTUROUS WOMEN

In Edwardian days, the term "adventuress" was frequently used as a euphemism for a woman who went out to get the man or men she wanted and enjoyed sex with them, regardless of what the world thought about her. She was highly selective in choosing her partner or partners, and equally selective about the nature and intimacy of the favors she bestowed. The gifts she received seemed often disproportionate to the amount of sexual and social favor given and she was often a woman of independent and decisive personality.

The description just given fits our own sample of sexually adventurous women remarkably well, always allowing that the number of men on whom they have bestowed their attentions is in some cases no more than one. A few of these women are professional "mistresses," a term we prefer to the traditional one because in fact they seldom give actual intercourse for money. Instead, they create (as do their nonprofessional sisters) theaters of fantasy in which they and their partner can act out a ritual which very likely both of them enjoy. This is in fact the interesting differentiator: very rarely does this type of professional conform to the stereotype of the conventional hooker bored with her work and serving up a bland collage of sexual variations with as much emotion as a butcher serving up a portion of lamb chops. Instead, they take much genuine enjoyment in what they do, mocking themselves with the strange, half-praising, half-denigrating label of "superbitch" and seeming to ride the tiger of their sexual ebullience with laconic amusement.

In a while we will examine this group in terms of the questionnaires used throughout this book; for the moment, the following case history may give at least a flavor of the professional in this group.

Jean E. is thirty-five years old, a "business lady" who caters entirely to masochists and transvestites. She states that she enjoys her work and that her sadistic activities are real in the sense that only to a small extent is she putting on an act for the benefit of her clients. Jean comes of Russo-Polish immigrant stock and has an attractive voice. Her speech, in spite of her working-class background, is without accent. Her mother was deserted by her husband soon after Jean's birth and was apparently extremely neurotic. Soon after developing Parkinson's disease in her late fifties, she committed suicide by drug overdose.

Jean was brought up "within the family," as she puts it; the war was on, and grandmother, uncle, aunt, mother, two sisters and Jean were evacuated to the country. When the air raids lessened in intensity, however, the family returned to London. Jean went to

live with her grandparents, while the mother and two sisters lived
and worked on the other side of the city. Jean went to visit them
every weekend. "Though the atmosphere was not happy," she
comments, "I was resented right from the start. My mother had
had an affair during the war, though it was never talked about. A
week after my mother died, I asked my uncle who my father was,
and he gave me a name. Almost relieved, I rang my sister to tell
her the news, and she said, 'But which Mr. X.—the father or one
of the six sons?' So I still don't know. I doubt actually whether
anyone wanted me. Grandma would say, 'I'll send you to your
mother!' when I was bad. And my mother was terrible—I remember my sisters dragging me into the bathroom and locking the door
while mother foamed and hammered away at the door when she
got mad. And mother used to say, 'If you're not a good girl, I'll
send you to your father.' Meanwhile, my sisters resented me at
that age because they had to travel across town every Friday to
pick me up and bring me home, then again on Sunday to take me
back. Mind you, I can't say that I blame them, for they were
grown up and had lives of their own to lead. We get on all right
now, though."

Jean developed normally except for spasms of bedwetting and
nightmares in which everything and everyone except her grandmother was seething with black flies. These nightmares, with the
same images, recurred at a much later date during a nervous breakdown. She attended primary school without incident, scraped into
junior high, but left at fifteen with no qualifications, in spite of
being a "teacher's pet" and showing great skill at drawing and
painting. She had learned little of sex at that time—even menstrua-
tion came to her as a surprise and a scare.

On leaving school, she did a "couple of useless jobs," as she
puts it. "I kept running away from home. I was your average juve-
nile delinquent," she adds cheerfully, "hanging around fair-
grounds, West End jazz clubs and dives. Then I got sent to reform
school by my mom on the grounds that I was uncontrollable, in
need of care and attention and so on. Mind you, I kept on abscond-
ing from there, too. On one of these occasions I met my first husband. I was outside the door of a pool hall in Soho trying to sell
some dresses I'd stolen from my mother's place, and he offered to
buy them. 'Bring 'em around to my place, gal,' he said and,
whoosh! I was abducted! I hardly saw daylight for about six
months. And then one day, zoomph, I was out on the streets."

Jean's first husband had been a pimp for some years, although
she was put into his care and custody after being declared out of
parental control; the authorities apparently had taken no steps to

find out anything about him. She learned "just about everything" about sex from him; before that, although she was not a virgin, she had regarded sex as "just one of those things a fella did to you." At no stage, in fact, did she ever have any prudishness or reticence about accepting any particular facet of sex, masturbation, homosexuality or any other form of eroticism. Even now, she regards herself as bisexual—a fact she seems to have discovered almost inadvertently while putting on a lesbian show for clients and finding that she enjoyed it.

Ten months after her marriage she had a child which did not live and one year later she had a boy. She was still a prostitute, and described, almost idly, the highly unsatisfactory life she was leading, attempting to bring up her child and deal with a fair number of clients. She was already well versed in catering to "particular requirements," and while acting as "maid" to another woman, she realized that acting the sexual dominant had advantages, in that she had more control of the situation, within the rules governing this type of fantasy—she no longer needed to have intercourse, and could charge higher fees.

"And my social life improved," Jean continues. "It's not that the upper classes are more into kinky fantasies, but they're the only ones that can afford to have them played out properly!" At this stage she gets out her scrap book, and it is evident from the number of "compromising photos" of people that she possesses that her circle of clients is indeed wide and includes a number of fairly well-known people in the political, business and entertainment world.

"What you must realize," she goes on, "is that once you have a client who wants a particular scene with you, it isn't just a case of come-and-go in fifteen minutes. You might have dinner, see a show, then back to my place to act out a fantasy lasting a couple of hours. You get to know a guy in that time, and you stand much more chance of having regulars. You'll know about their wives, kids, jobs, everything." This type of attitude indicates that Jean's relationship with many of her clients extends beyond the business of sex, in whatever form she portrays it. Never, she says, has she used her position for blackmail purposes, "largely because I can make money with less hassle by what I normally do than by all the paraphernalia of threats," she says with disarming candor.

Jean carries out virtually any fantasy that her clients wish, though naturally there are some that she finds more pleasant than others. She will get them to describe their desired scenario, then reinterpret it to suit her own wishes and the props she possesses. She has a miniature dungeon, a very large wardrobe of sex garments, an equally large trunk full of "props," instruments of so-called punishment, bondage equipment and the like. Transvestites may need no more than her company and assistance with cross-dressing while for an hour or so they escape into femininity. "I hardly do a thing," says Jean, "except provide them with a place to be what they want to be without any worry."

Jean's second marriage was no more successful than the first. Her second husband was a sexual sadist within our definition of the term, namely, that his sadistic acts with Jean were developed carefully and tacitly agreed to by both of them. Jean now has a fine taste for these activities. She was, however, also on drugs (both hard and soft); her husband belonged to the criminal world, and his imprisonment on a bank robbery charge wrecked the marriage. Jean cites with pride the fact that she has cured herself of heroin addiction, though she still takes softer drugs at intervals. She has manic and depressive moods, has had two nervous breakdowns and has attempted suicide at least twice.

Yet in spite of this sad side to her life, Jean is, as far as we can judge, the sort of person who can cope. She is in group therapy, is planning for her retirement from the profession, determined to quit before things get too tough. She attends evening classes in a number of subjects, and has a fair number of friends who have little to do with her business life. Part of this attitude of survival undoubtedly stems from an almost näive acceptance of the experiences of life, an attitude which serves her well in her work. No fantasy is too outrageous, foolish, childish or complex for her to play out, and she has come to enjoy just about everything that she does sexually. Unlike many ladies of her calling, she does not despise her clients, however much she may "dominate" them. In fact, she makes few value judgments about people and their behavior in any sphere, and even in her depressed moods seems more cast down by the illogicality of the world and those that inhabit it than by the good and bad of the matter.

To what extent is Jean typical of the professional superbitch class? We believe that in fact she represents its major characteristics very well. The aggressive mother and absent father pattern which has traditionally supposed to have been the hallmark of the social deviant, the troubled adolescence and the effects of the environment often summed up by the social worker's report of "bad family upbringing," the above-average intelligence and creativity (Jean is an accomplished artist in watercolors), the outgoing attitude which, as we have seen, contrasts with the often more introverted personality associated with her clients—all these seem to reflect the group in general. Jean also displays the enjoyment of many forms of sexual activity typical of the group—an eclecticism which may be surprising to those who have noted the comparatively limited themes of pleasure particular to the other groups.

Let it not be thought, however, that Jean's poor family background is a necessary requisite of the high priestess of the temple of male sex fantasies. The case history of Caroline E. proves that it is not.

Caroline E. has little more than a disliked stepfather in her upbringing to qualify as having a "poor family situation." Her development was unexceptional, her relationship with her mother was excellent and that with her younger siblings unremarkable. Her childhood and adolescent environment were definitely stable and apparently untinged with trauma, although she remembers, suddenly and with some surprise, that she used to beat her dolls when she was a child. She learned about sex at fourteen, first tried intercourse at eighteen and enjoyed it. Her early adulthood was uninhibited but not delinquent. Her first real introduction to sadomasochism was via a boyfriend who enjoyed being beaten by women. This was later followed by a visit (with the same boyfriend, who set up the scenario) to a "madam" so that they might use her equipment for a sadomasochistic session, and the madam's subsequent invitation to Caroline to help with some of the other clients. These experiences confirmed in her an attitude which she found, and still finds, pleasurable and exciting.

Caroline describes her pleasure in sadomasochistic activities as not directly sexual, more a mental kick, like being high after a few drinks. She has an unexpectedly high opinion of her clients, in spite of the universally submissive role that they wish to take. She describes them as "intelligent, sensitive, mostly well-bred—and even when they are not well-bred, they have a kindness and gentleness which I think is very attractive." She believes that love and sadomasochistic behavior can go together without difficulty "because any relationship develops unspoken rules about what the participants do and do not do, just like me and my clients." We were reminded by her of Jean in one probably quite important aspect: both women appear to have a complete absence of any system of value judgments which they might apply to their clients' sexual behavior. However unusual the fantasy, neither girl would spend more than a passing moment in considering whether they would or would not like to service that fantasy, nor whether or not they ought to do so.

An examination of the data from the Sex Fantasy Questionnaire for this group in fact immediately confirms that our sexually adventurous women are more than merely sadomasochistically inclined, as the source of contact that we had with them might imply. Rather, they are almost anything-inclined, Table 16 showing them to have a higher fantasy rating than an age-matched control group of females on all but three of the forty themes examined. It is important to remember that this is a rating of frequency of fantasy. Although we may expect a higher *activity* rating on all themes if our group is highly "professionally" oriented, the high fantasy ratings confirm that the group's high enjoyment of most sexual themes is genuine and is not merely a byproduct of what they get out of sex materially.

Of course it could be argued that if fantasy and activity are correlated (as we have known to be the case), and activity is materially rewarded, then both activity and fantasy ratings may rise. As one nineteen-year-old prostitute said to us, "The sight of money literally makes me feel sexy." However, we are assured by several members of the group that sexiness and material reward are for them little connected. Even when only the responses of known professionals are taken into account, their rating of the degree to which their sadomasochistic activities were geared to material or financial reward averaged only 3.66 out of a possible 5—only a little more than "partly; a gift is nice."

Table 16. **Percentage of fantasy output within sexually adventurous (dominant) women and controls assigned to each of four main categories.**

	Intimate themes	Exploratory themes	Impersonal themes	Sadomasochistic themes
Dominant women	34.1	20.4	20.7	24.8
Age-matched female controls	51.0	19.8	17.2	12.0

If, however, we break the ratings down into Intimate, Exploratory, Impersonal and Sadomasochistic categories—as was done in the case of our other variant groups—it becomes clear that this group does have a bias away from intimate fantasies and slightly toward exploratory themes, more toward impersonal themes and most toward sadomasochistic themes (see Table 16). It is these themes that form our next point of interest.

Before proceeding, however, to the discussion of individual themes, we might do well to examine the relationship between total fantasy rating, used as a measure of libido, and the average rating of overtly sadistic and masochistic themes for this group and for its control group. In Chaper 4 we postulated that for males, as libido rises, the ratings of masochistic fantasy generally grow at a higher rate than those of sadistic fantasy. Is this true for women as well? Remembering that we are working with smaller female groups than the male ones previously studied, and that therefore our conclusions must be somewhat more tentative than we would have liked, we can see from Figure 8 that our findings confirm the hypothesis and so it may be extended to cover both sexes. The interesting theoretical implications of these results will be discussed in the final chapter.

What individual themes in our Sex Fantasy Questionnaire interest this group more than they do the female control group? All but three of them do to some extent and at least half of them to a statistically significant degree. Intercourse with an anonymous stranger, threesomes and orgies, all the sadomasochistic themes, receiving oral sex (the *only* theme in the intimate category), being excited by material or clothing, mate-swapping, excitement from watching urination, sex with someone much older or much younger, seducing—and being seduced as—an innocent, having sex with someone of a different race, using objects for stimulation and viewing erotica all serve to distinguish between the sexually adventurous women and the control group.

Two points are of special interest here. The first is the virtual absence of intimate themes as differentiators between the

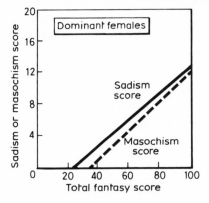
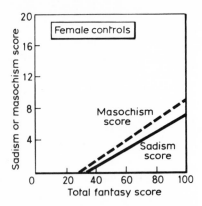

Figure 8. Sadism and masochism scores related to total fantasy output within each female group, variant and control. Each line is a line of best fit through the appropriate scattergram. Note that, as with the male groups, the masochistic or submissive fantasies increase in frequency faster than do sadistic or aggressive fantasies as total fantasy output rises.

groups. Cunnilingus is traditionally the means by which the professional "mistress" rewards her "slave" at the conclusion of such role-playing, and we see no reason why this activity should be confined to professionals in such a situation, so whether this particular activity should be called intimate within this context is doubtful. However, one should not castigate this group for failing to show higher ratings than the control group for intimate themes, since the absence of sizeable difference is due not to low ratings by the sexually adventurous women but to high ratings by their more conventional sisters in the control group.

The second point to note is the high average ratings of these adventurous women on the fetishistic theme of being excited by material or clothing. This is interesting because fetishism in females is thought to be extremely rare, both from clinical observation and theory, and from the point of view of male fetishists themselves, who have long bemoaned their inability to find similarly fetishistic partners. Admittedly there is nowadays cited a number of examples of women who enjoy, and get sexually turned on by, fetishistic activities. So should we describe our Superbitches as fetishists? Probably not, for their average rating on the fetishism item of 1.64 (compared with 0.80 for control males and 0.25 for control females) reflects the level expected in a group which, rewarded materially, emotionally or behaviorally for playing the partner's tune in terms of costume, begins to turn on to the costume or the accompanying activity in itself. They do not really compare with our "true" fetishists, who after all have shown a mean rating of over 4.0 on the item relating to their predilection.

When we turn to the demographic and attitudinal self-ratings shown by this group on our questionnaire (Table 15), it is perhaps surprising how small the differences are between the "superbitch" and control groups. The sexually adventurous woman is less often married, but her satisfaction with her partner, if she has a steady one, appears rather greater than that of her control counterpart. She self-rates her sex life as a little more satisfactory, has a slightly higher frequency of orgasm, a slightly higher self-rated sex drive, a somewhat greater number of partners, a fractionally less permissive upbringing, slightly less sexual inhibition and a slightly lower estimated frequency of punishment as a child, but the differences are not significant. Incidentally, it might be helpful to point out to those who expected the professional element within this group to have raised the average rating for orgasm frequency far higher than the case appears to be, that, first, a professional seldom has an orgasm if she has intercourse with a client, and, second, professionals catering to sex patterns such as those treated in this book seldom have intercourse with their clients anyway. In fact, we learn from interviews that the only time that this type of professional is likely to enjoy orgasms is while "rewarding" a masochistic client by commanding him to perform cunnilingus on her for an extended period of time.

With regard to the question of punishment and sexual behavior, the absence of a higher punishment frequency in our special group may conceal a more interesting finding. We observed in Chapter 6 that among males there is virtually no

connection between the estimated frequency of corporal punishment in childhood and the frequency of either intimate or
sadomasochistic fantasies. Nor did experience of punishment
relate to sadistic or masochistic fantasies measured separately.
When we turn to the female group, however, it appears that a
very powerful association exists between punishment frequency and the incidence of both intimate and sadistic (but
not masochistic) themes. Speculation as to why these particular categories of fantasy should correlate with punishment
may be fruitless, although one could make a case for the idea
that, following a history of punishment, the female tries to
obtain either loving reassurance or vengeance on encounter-
ing the "aggressive" sexual approach of the male. The fact
that the female may have been punished by a female when
young, as much as by a man, need not stand in the way of such
a theory, for we have found a very high correlation (0.46) between punishment and homosexual (lesbian) activity for this
group.

It is rather more interesting to ask why these correlations
should occur for females and not for males. We have no defin-
itive evidence to offer on this point, but it has been suggested
(West, 1967) that adolescent and preadolescent males who get
into trouble with the law generally do so for offences not involving sexual behavior and seldom for offences with a sexual
connotation. Adolescent girls, however, are more often in
trouble as a result of sexually oriented activities, and indeed
are sometimes placed into care at a younger age because they
are regarded as more exposed to sexual danger than boys.
Does the correlation between punishment and fantasy only
occur when the behavior that is punished has itself some sexual connotation? It is not clear from classical learning theory
how this connection would be expected to occur, but the associations can be very complex.

It is interesting to note how well the personality findings
confirm the "adventuress" stereotype. On the psychoticism
scale, our sexually adventurous women easily beat both the
male and female control groups for toughness, scoring very
significantly above the average for either control group. In

terms of extraversion, their average is again higher than the controls. Although with the small numbers involved in this group the difference fails to reach statistical significance, it seems that they frequently offer to their men an outgoing and impulsive attitude that can usefully counterbalance the more introspective and shy traits typical of the male masochist. In a lasting relationship the man in question may form a useful, if occasionally infuriating, anchor for the more ebullient female.

With respect to neuroticism, the "superbitch" type is more emotional than her male counterpart, but only a shadow more so than her control-group sister. However, if we examine the data from only the professionals within this group, remembering that these professionals frequently advertise themselves within the pages of their special magazines as creatures of tempestuous and unpredictable mood, the emotionality figure for this group rises sharply and becomes significantly higher than even their nonprofessional sisters.

The stereotype of the sexually adventurous women is further confirmed in the lie-scale figures. Whatever the interpretation of this scale (a tendency to lie, a need for social acceptance, a measure of conservatism), our adventuresses show that they would rather "tell the truth and shame the devil," disdain the power of social pressure and have little regard for the establishment view. Their average score is the lowest among all the groups that we have studied. And, for what it is worth, the members of the professional subgroup have a lower average figure still.

We have now finished our survey of male and female variant and control groups. Not everything that we have found has been expected, nor have we made much of an attempt to explain why a set of sexual behaviors, which even many of our variant subjects admit is somewhat strange, should have claimed them with such intensity and permanence. In the final chapter we shall attempt to place the findings within a framework of theory and discuss what has been learned about the acquisition of sexual behavior.

8

Conclusions and
Implications

When we started the work that has formed the substance of this book, we had no particular axe to grind. We had neither a wish to condemn variants or their activities as sick, sinful or sinister, nor a desire to conduct a campaign which with the aid of a gloss of scientific respectability sought to advocate variant behavior as being especially desirable. We were instead perhaps a little puzzled by the fact that when so many ordinary people have found extreme pleasure in the intimacy of conventional lovemaking, a number of men should actively pursue and even prefer an inanimate object, a ritual of apparent pain and humiliation or an imitation of the opposite gender in order to achieve sexual pleasure. We have learned from clinical reports that certain attributes of personality were commonly associated with those who found these alternative sexual patterns burdensome enough to seek relief from them, but we did not know whether the unconventional sex pattern produced the dissonance of personality or vice versa. As a result, we believed that it might help in the understanding of the development of sexual patterns to study those who practiced variant behaviors without finding them a source of dismay or unease.

What, then, have we discovered about such people? In some respects, we believe that they have shown themselves to be like script-writers and actors in rather specialized plays, put on in the theater of fantasy which all of us possess. Let us consider this analogy.

In the entertainment world, a fair number of people are much involved in the creation and presentation of plays, films or television performances. Most writers use fairly standard situations in their plots, recipes of proven success that everyone understands, twists of plot that may be novel but which seem perfectly logical and need little interpretation when played out. The stories generally are based on experiences in the writers' own lives, but they portray activities with which almost everyone can identify. The characters are fairly stereotyped—breadwinner or nurturer, parent or child, conformist or rebel—and as a result, they are easy to accept. The actors find it easy to take up their roles, and are likely to enjoy playing their parts even after many performances, discovering that the rewards outweigh the boredom which might be expected to set in when many repetitive performances are called for. Those that provide the setting and the props find the task easy and the stage management minimal: almost any theater can provide the necessary setting.

By contrast, a rather smaller number of people have a more specialized involvement in the world of theatrical or cinematic presentation. Such people feel a driving force within them that compels them to portray some unique inner message that they feel must be given formal shape. The writers concerned are aware that their message may not be of interest or intelligible to a mass audience, but they have just as compelling a desire to communicate themselves to the world about them as has the more conventional writer. The theme of the production is less conventional than those normally portrayed, the twists of plot more complex, their nature such that, to avoid censure, they need to be portrayed symbolically rather than directly. While the plot develops as logically and inevitably as those in the mass-entertainment market, it may appear so unusual that its logic is less easily understood. Once more the stories will largely be based upon experiences in the writers' past lives, but the message may be less universal, more urgent and generally more serious in content. The characters may perhaps be as stereotyped as those found in the more popular type of production, but are often cruder, more cartoon-like in concept—macho or over-feminine, torturer or victim, witch-mother and child, peacock or nonentity. The actors, if not contentedly accepting a type-casting which they themselves resemble, may find it difficult to play their parts without tension, may find the longer runs repetitively boring, and may leave the play unless the salary is extremely high. The setting and props that are called for may only emphasize the bizarreness of the plot, yet without such aids the performance may become meaningless and fundamentally impossible. In some cases, it may need to be put on at a specially designed or equipped theater.

The world of love and sex has considerable parallels with this theatrical world, given that the activities and attendant emotions are—or should be—real and not merely a game. Nearly all of us are engaged in the presentation of plays of love. Many utilize fairly standard ways of expressing affection and sexual desire, recipes which time and society's pressures have shown as being easily and widely understood as well as leading to happy results. The roles played may be fairly stereotyped—lover and loved, father-figure and child-bride, queen and courtier, coquette and stud—and are consequently easy to accept and play. The participants will not find it difficult to give the other what he or she desires, and are likely to enjoy playing their parts even after many performances, finding that the rewards outweigh the boredom of apparent repetitiveness. Setting and props will have only marginal influence, for conventional love and sex can be expressed in more or less any private situation.

By contrast, a rather smaller number of people, as in the

theatrical analogy, feel that driving force within them that pushes them to act out a different, more specialized inner message. They are aware that those with whom they interact may not understand, but their desire to communicate this theme is stronger for being so seldom understood or accepted. The analogy of the less conventional theme, the more complex plot and the use of symbolism in order to avoid censure even perhaps from themselves, holds true. The plot will in fact be as logical as those played out in conventional lovemaking, but it may appear so unusual that it thus seems illogical to the uncommitted. As before, the plots will fundamentally be based upon an experience or experiences in the creator's life, but may be mutated as a result of familial or social conditioning. The characters are sexually stereotyped—macho or over-feminine, torturer or victim, bitch-goddess or slave, peacock or nonentity. Those with whom the variant interacts may find it difficult to participate without tension or eventual boredom, and may refuse to cooperate unless paid as a professional. The setting and props may only emphasize the bizarreness of this form of love and passion, yet without attention to them, sexual performance may be fundamentally impossible. As a result, the specialist may have to have access to a specially equipped setting.

The theatrical analogy will serve us as a framework for summarizing what has been learned from the studies presented in this book and from the people with whom we have talked during interviews and less formal conversations. In spite of its less manageable nature, the richness of the latter source of data has persuaded us to use it in our summaries.

WRITING THE SCRIPT

After casting himself in the central role of the script, the sexual variant creates characters based on family, friends, sexual partners and other significant persons whom he has met, but uses more "voices from the past" than the nonvariant. He starts work on his script when very young and continues to develop and refine it throughout his life.

We are of course not arguing that the development of variant behavior is entirely a matter of learning a behavior or a fantasy directly from childhood experiences: our tentative twin-study in fact indicates that transvestism and, to a lesser extent, sadomasochism have a genetic component to them. However, it is clear that learning has a great deal to do with the acquisition of variant behavior. The unusually strong femininity in the transvestite and the unusually strong aggressiveness or, more often, submissiveness in the sadomasochist may be partly genetic, but the nature of the expression of those traits must be a matter of learning. The question posed in one sex magazine, "Where were all the vinyl fetishists before vinyl was invented?" spotlights the twin channels of predisposition and learning. The answer "they were busy being fetishistic over something else" is not based on scientific evidence but illustrates the popular belief that the fetishist is predisposed to variant behavior, while learning determines what form his predilection shall take.

Our personality studies have shown that variants in general tend to be more introverted than people whose sexual behavior is more conventional. Introverts are more easily conditioned than extraverts; they are more sensitive to stimuli and acquire stronger emotional associations. Therefore, they are perhaps more likely to turn on to *any* sexual association (remember that the variant generally has more fantasies than the average individual and fantasies grow well in the soil of associations and images), but the more conventional sexual associations probably get "blocked off" by parental or societal injunctions. Learning thus plays an especially important part in the development of the variant's script, and the process by which it occurs must be described in some detail—even if only because it is the question most frequently asked by variants themselves.

The process cannot be described in isolation, however, because buried in the question "How is variant behavior learned?" lies also the additional puzzle of "If variant behavior is a matter of learning, why is it that women don't learn it as easily as men?" Here, two fundamental differences between men and women may help us to postulate the answer. Let us take the simplest case, that of the development of the rubber fetish. Here, the original stimulus bears a very close relation, if not an exact similarity, to the resulting predilection. In other cases, the resultant liking is different from the original stimulus but the two will bear a symbolic, if not factual, relationship to one another.

Fetishism has about it a particular element which makes it stand out from conventional behavior: its visual focus. A fetish fabric, object or garment usually cries with considerable force, "Look at me!" Often black against lighter tones, frequently shiny or iridescent, theatrically overemphasizing either its more modest presentation in fashion or the part of the female body with which it is associated, it proclaims its existence almost as if it had a voice of its own. Now a number of studies in perception have suggested that men are more sensitive to visual stimuli than women: as a result, they might be more likely to pick up and internalize a stimulus that by its nature obtrudes upon the consciousness under circumstances in which it might otherwise not be noticed. For example, one does not generally notice feet; nevertheless, among a number of feet walking down a street, those clad in eye-catching footwear—high heels, high boots and thin-strap sandals for the women, cowboy boots for the men—will be preferentially noticed. The men might notice this attention-catching footwear more than the women, and unless they are homosexually inclined will probably notice the female footwear far more readily than that worn by their own sex. In fact, this visual sensitivity of males may be confined to certain areas of interest (women, for example, observe more details about babies than do men) but it certainly applies to the domain of sexual attraction (see Wilson and Nias, 1976).

Much initial learning seems to follow the model of classical conditioning, to which the variant appears to be more susceptible than the nonvariant. Classical conditioning occurs when the stimulus to be learned and reacted to is paired with another stimulus which already has an emotional accompaniment. Repeated pairing allies the reaction originally associated with the old stimulus to the new one. However, for any pairing to take place in the everyday world rather than in the laboratory, where the relevant stimuli are impressed fairly firmly upon the subject, the stimulus has to be noticed. The more easily the stimulus impresses itself upon the attention, and the more easily one notices stimuli anyway, the more chance there is that a new conditioned emotional response will be formed. There is, of course, more to it than that, but for the moment we can allow that males form such pairings, reacting to them with an arousal response, more easily than do females, and that the variant-to-be will form them most frequently of all, and preferentially with those materials or objects that for one reason or another are visually compelling.

A second factor which may predispose men more than women toward acquiring a fetish (or, indeed, toward acquiring almost any form of variant behavior as well as a conventional sex pattern) involves the mechanism of biofeedback. Biofeedback is the summation of all the messages, small and large, that the body sends back to the brain as to what it is doing and what it feels. Some of these messages are easily noticeable, as when we touch a hot kettle and a very powerful and painful message races back to the brain. A lot more of the little messages about ourselves are much more difficult to recognize consciously, however, unless we train ourselves to do so by having them transduced and perhaps amplified by an electronic machine so that a greater amount of information is passed back to us. By such means, we can learn to control certain aspects of our bodily functions which were previously thought to be beyond our control. Believe it or not, a person can thus learn to raise their blood pressure in one ear above that in the other.

When it comes to information about whether we are sexually aroused or not, males (even when very young) have a very good biofeedback amplifier, namely, their own penises. No particular part of a woman's body, sex organs or otherwise, gives such an immediate, definite and noticeable reaction; any reaction she does have to arousal is more diffuse, occurring in the clitoris, the vagina, the nipples, the back, the ear lobes and almost any erogenous zone. Because the reaction is more diffuse and less predictable, it is more easily overlooked, and the clear message of "I am excited" does not as easily register in her conscious mind. Of course, it may do so eventually in the sense that the woman's learning may be slower but more general, leading to her being turned on by a *situation* such as "a romantic atmosphere and a considerate man" while the male would be more likely to be aroused by the more defined *image* of, say, a nineteen-year-old blonde in black stockings and garters. It is also as well to remember that the arousal produced by stimulus messages received by a woman is somewhat more susceptible to hormonal influences which can heighten or lessen her receptivity and thereby alter the efficacy of the learning process.

The other concept that must be understood in this context is that of arousal. It is quite possible that as far as the learning process is concerned, the arousal which occurs as the result of environmental *or* random internal stimulation need not be directly sexual at all, but may be just the general state of being awake or aware, which can change from minute to minute. To some extent the body, as opposed to the mind, has difficulty in distinguishing one form of arousal from another; as a result, any strong emotion can be translated in the mind, under appropriate conditions, into sexual arousal, which is nearly always judged pleasant. Some famous experiments by Stanley Schachter of Stanford University have shown that the effects of adrenalin—a general stimulant—may be described by subjects as fear, anger or even love, depending on their expectations and the social circumstances prevailing at the time.

Let us now put these concepts together to trace the course of events which lead to the learning of a fetishistic script. The model contains assumptions, admittedly, but they are assumptions for which there is a reasonable amount of experimental support.

At some point, the young child is at a high level of arousal. This high arousal can occur purely fortuitously, in the way that every parent has seen happen when a child switches his mood for no better reason than his chemical switches happened to be set that way at that moment. On the other hand, the arousal peak can be due to anger, discomfort, pleasure, warmth, security, mother-being-absent or mother-taking-active-interest (and, incidentally, this is probably why no experience common to all can be said to initiate the learning of a fetish: it isn't always feeding, bath-time, bedwetting or spanking, it's anything that goes with high arousal). At that moment, there is also present an element of the fetish-material-to-be: apron, baby pants, crib sheet, mackintosh-as-shield-from-rain-and-cold. The male child notices the stimulus more readily than the female and connects it with the high arousal state, which may or may not have any direct sexual connotation about it but in any case is recorded in the genital area by a minor tumescence. The message recorded merely says at this stage, "Possible link between *that* material and *that* excited feeling." The youngster is in fact making a miniature scientific hypothesis that certain qualities in a fabric are associated with a particular feeling.

When the fabric turns up again, the child remembers the previous association and says, in effect, "Let me test my hypothesis by searching for that feeling." Unfortunately he often makes a mistake which is common in all of us. If he notices no excitement, his verdict is "not proven, but my hypothesis may still be right," simply because nobody likes to admit, even to themselves, that they are wrong. If he does feel excitement— even coincidentally, or because he expected it and therefore he felt it—his verdict is that the hypothesis has been proved. An expectancy is thus strengthened that "next time it will work the same way" and confirmation is almost bound to be obtained on subsequent occasions because the reaction becomes a self-fulfilling prophecy.

During this testing process, the male child will notice that his penis is almost certainly the best place from which to pick up a message concerning his excited state. The female child, failing to feel such a definite and localized response, is more likely to dismiss the connection between fetish object and arousal state, even if she has noticed the possibility of such an association in the first place. As a result, she forgets the whole thing, and the fetish script is never properly read, let alone learned.

Whether the male child regards the feeling in his penis as sexual, in the sense that he knows what the word means, is at this stage irrelevant. The point is that later, when overtly sexual stimuli produce virtually the same feeling in his penis, he will classify the fetishistic association as a sexual one even if the original association had nothing sexual about it whatever.

Of course, the fetishistic script is by no means the only one concerning sex that the child is learning. He may also learn scripts linking pleasure and woman, less pleasure and man— or even, in some cases, the reverse. He may learn conditional scripts which say "girls are only pleasure-giving if you do a lot for them," or "females are only pleasure-giving if you force them to be so." Armed, then, with a number of script-lines or hypotheses, any of which might be true, the child moves toward adolescence, to a time when he is going to be able to try out both variant scripts (called by clinicians "faulty learning") and conventional scripts within a directly sexual context.

So far we have not mentioned anxiety, the favorite explanatory tool of the therapeutic explanation-giver. This is not to say that we deny the power of anxiety to cause trouble for the person with problems of any kind. What is crucial, however, is whether one regards the higher neuroticism of the variant as being the *result* of his variant behavior or the partial reason for it. Even if anxiety is merely regarded as one more classification for arousal, its power is such that the higher emotionality of the variant-to-be will help produce an especially high response to the fetishistic stimulus, thus strengthening its "power." If, however, anxiety is regarded as the result of early learning, then, as our results have confirmed, variant sexual behavior is more likely to develop in individuals whose up-bringing has been restrictive, which usually means based on fear and guilt-induction. We shall see this factor arise again in the next section.

WHY IS THE SCRIPT RETAINED?

As the child grows up, he may receive messages from his parents, potential partners or anyone who he believes to be influential in his life, to the effect that the usual target for his genital feelings (i.e., the female *per se,* and particularly her vagina) is forbidden, or naughty or wicked, or dirty, or unmen-tionable or in some other way not to be approached. Now, because he is more easily conditioned than most, he takes these messages seriously and believes in them more easily: because of his higher emotionality, his attempts to disobey the messages lead to overpowerful anxiety and guilt associ-ated with his arousal. In seeking to obtain sexual pleasure when aroused, he may therefore remember that the fetish fab-ric gave pleasure without interaction with the female. He therefore reaches for the mackintosh or whatever he can find that is similar and naturally receives no off-putting message about "forbidden sexual object" because inanimate objects don't transmit any message—except that this one produces arousal as it always did, purely by conditioning. Orgasm then results, confirming that, for that boy, having a mackintosh is better than having a girl since it produces less anxiety and more pleasure. Without the presence of girls who can produce alternative hypotheses to test, such as "Mary Jones sends me powerful signals that she (and maybe even her vagina) is not a forbidden target" or "girls are pleasure-giving even if one does no more than kiss and cuddle them," the fetish habit may become virtually all-powerful—especially if girls are scarce. On the other hand, if there are sufficient Mary Joneses about, and the pleasure they afford the young man in one way or another is greater than that hitherto associated with the fetish object, then adherence to the fetish will either die away or, more often, remain at a level far below that which would predispose him to consider himself fetishistic.

The model that we have so far presented is, we feel, the simplest that fits the realities of fetish development. A simple model of classical conditioning cannot alone explain why males are more prone to developing variant behavior than are females. Neither can it tell us why it is that variancy occurs in only a small percentage of the population. After all, we are all quite likely to register some form of highly noticeable object associated with the female at a time when we are randomly highly aroused. On a simple classical-conditioning basis, it would appear that we should all have a fetish of some kind, if we are male, and therefore some kind of unusual or restrictive upbringing needs to be postulated in addition.* This, of course, is the theme of Desmond Morris's book *The Human Zoo*—human sexual behavior is in many ways more reminiscent of caged animals than animals in the wild.

The model is, however, probably not complete. Variant behavior is often more complex than merely "being aroused by the fetish object," even when one is nominally a fetishist. Readers will remember the frequency with which one variation is allied to another, and recalling either the many fantasies in popular sex magazines or, for example, the favorite sex dream of Mr. C. in Chapter 6, will note the multiplicity of themes present in a single fantasy. No single childhood experience could directly serve as a basis for classical conditioning for such fantasies.

On the basis of clinical examination of the fantasies and behavior of sexual deviants, McGuire and associates (1965) developed the idea that actual experience may merely supply a fantasy for use during masturbation. Whenever the fantasy is

---

* On the other hand, if a fetish was endemic in the male population it would probably not be recognized as such. Could we say that interest in female breasts is a universal male fetish? Only if it became exclusive, detached or greatly exaggerated would we consider invoking the term "breast fetish."

used under such circumstances, the conditioned link with the pleasure of orgasm is strengthened and it becomes progressively more exciting. What is more, since the fantasy is subject to the usual laws and limitations of memory, it becomes modified over time. Certain aspects of the precipitating experience may be forgotten and others accentuated. Additional appropriate plots may be borrowed from other sources, images invented, subplots introduced, and all of these tried out for effectiveness in providing additional interest and pleasure. The process is, in fact, very similar to that used by any playwright in the construction of his play. As McGuire points out, the fact that boys masturbate more than girls may also help to explain the preponderance of male variancy—or rather their tendency to fixate on certain visual configurations, whether conventional or unconventional.

Another finding of McGuire and his colleagues supports the idea that in order for a variant behavior to be retained, a block (real or imagined) on conventional sexual outlets must be present. More than half of McGuire's patients believed that a normal sex life was not possible for them. Such beliefs were connected with overly strict upbringing, guilt, unfortunate early experiences with girls and feelings of physical or social inadequacy. Our finding that the restrictiveness of upbringing of our variant groups was slightly higher than that of the control group is consistent with that observation. True, the difference was somewhat less striking in our study, but then McGuire's subjects were patients seeking treatment for their condition and therefore not as happy about their situation as our subjects, who were seeking no assistance in the management of their predilections.

This theory that a variant fantasy or behavior is shaped and altered by trial and error after a basic conditioning experience has occurred would help to explain the rather more elaborate themes inherent in sadomasochism, transvestism and certain other sexual variations not covered in this book. In sadomasochism the basic experience of being physically punished as a child, probably followed by a reassuring cuddle to show that

"Mommy loves you just the same, even when you're naughty," easily provides the conditioning model even though we were unable in our study to demonstrate that the simple frequency of punishment was important.* In transvestism the initiating association is most likely to be between high arousal and either the woman herself or the clothes she wears. In "true" transvestites, as opposed to the fetishistic variety, other influences, such as attractive female images which the child might believe were rewarding to imitate, would also contribute to the development of the feminized personality or role. We should not forget, however, the likelihood that powerful constitutional traits are also involved in true transvestism and transsexualism.

THE FETISH AS PROTOTYPE

We described the development of the fetish script in particular detail because it seems to be in some sense central to the three variations with which this book is concerned. For one thing it is the most commonly occurring of the three within both the normal and variant samples. Taking as a criterion a score of greater than two standard deviations above the mean rating on the relevant item in the Sex Fantasy Questionnaire, we found that our control group contained about 18 percent of men who could be considered fetishistic, but only around 2 to 5 percent who were transvestite or sadomasochistic. What this means is that a greater proportion of men in the general population are separated from the others with respect to a predilection of this kind, so as to form a little bump at the top end of the distribution of scores.

Then, if we look at the overlap in predilections among our

* There is no *a priori* reason why the absolute frequency of punishment should be the criterion of whether sadomasochistic behavior is learned by a conditioning process. It has often been shown that behaviors are effectively learned when the association between the old and the new stimulus only takes place intermittently.

major variant groups, we find that fetishism is central. There are more transvestites and sadomasochists with a fetishistic interest on top of their own predilection than there are transvestites interested in sadomasochism. This is seen quite clearly in Figure 9, which shows the extent to which the three groups overlap with each other. Note first that as many as 35 percent in any group have all three predilections. But whereas 64 percent of sadomasochists are also fetishists and 59 percent of transvestites are also fetishists, only 39 percent of sadomasochists are transvestites. What is more, if one subtracts from the latter those who are fetishistic we are reduced to only 4 percent of sadomasochists who are also transvestites—an almost perfect separation.

Fetishism, then, seems to mediate between the other variations. Each partakes of it as though it is in some way basic to

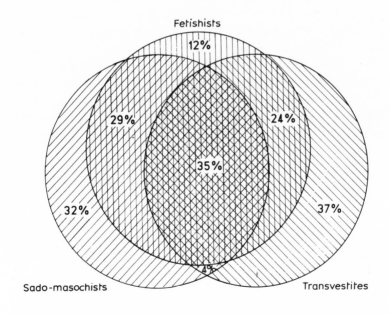

Figure 9. The overlap among male fetishist, transvestite and sadomasochist groups.

them. A probable reason for this is that sadomasochism and transvestism are very often outgrowths of, or elaborations upon, an early learned fetish. The conditioning of sexual excitement to an unusual object or event has served as the core to the full script that has been composed around it. By the time we reach sadomasochism and transvestite activities the fetish has become a prop or plot element that is used by a carefully selected cast of players, who are all acting in character with well-defined roles and relationships.

It is this full casting which makes it more difficult to mount an actual production and have the script acted out—there is a dearth of talented amateurs and union rates are high. As we have found in Chapter 4, the sadomasochist has particular difficulty in getting his script satisfactorily performed. The fetishist, on the other hand, can very often achieve satisfaction from a one-man show.

To sum up, then, it would seem that variant behavior is not the deliberate choice of the individual who is merely looking for some form of kick to satisfy his jaded sexual appetite. It is, rather, the logical though unfortunate reaction of a generally shy, introverted and emotionally over-sensitive child to a restrictive sexual upbringing. To the clinician, this may be nothing new; what is more interesting is its extension to those who find their variation actively enjoyable rather than burdensome.

CENSORSHIP OF THE PERFORMANCE

Many societies feel that it is necessary to exercise some form of control over the content of film, theatrical and other kinds of performance. Two particular areas of concern are those of sex and violence (Eysenck and Nias, 1979). The public, it seems, has rightly detected a biological connection between these two passions such that arousal in one area can lead to increased activity in the other. Yet there may be a sense in which the two are antagonistic, with the individual operating his own system of control over the more destructive instinct of aggression, at least within the context of love-making.

Let us recapitulate for a moment the findings set out in Chapters 4 and 6 concerning the differing rates of sadistic and masochistic fantasies as libido rises. We have studied eight groups of people—five male groups, one "between" group of transsexuals and two female groups. Both the male and the female groups included control and variant samples. In virtually all these groups it was found that, as libido—measured by total fantasy output—rises, submissive fantasies grow at a faster rate than do aggressive fantasies; only in the sadomasochistic group are the growth rates the same.

Our contention is that this is no accident or coincidence, but a state of affairs conducive to the survival of the species, given two assumptions which seem to us neither far-fetched nor illogical. The first of these is that fantasies are usually indicative of an attitude, so that if you create a sadistic fantasy it is because you feel sadistic, and if you create a submissive fantasy it is because you feel submissive. The second assumption is that what is true of the differences among individuals in the group is by and large true of the changes occurring within the individuals in that group. This of course is a weaker assumption and there are bound to be exceptions to the rule, but for the purposes of this argument we are going to assume that for most individuals it is true that, as his or her libido rises and falls according to circumstances, so the balance between aggressive and submissive impulses changes in sympathy. The net result is that, as sex desire rises, so the impulse in both sexes to *submit* rises faster than the desire to dominate or attack. Female readers will find this easy to accept; males, especially chauvinistic ones, may find it harder, though there is an honorable precedent for such a view in art, science and common knowledge. The Spaniard knows it from his country's proverb, "In love, neither command: both obey." The psychologist, in the shape of Barclay and Haber (1965) and Barclay alone (1971), showed that when people were put on the defensive by a member of the opposite sex who attacked them verbally, they reacted by producing *sexual* imagery more than aggressive. Folk wisdom has long accepted that women are frequently aroused by aggressive men, while a quick survey of certain television series, films or popular books (*Modesty Blaise, The Avengers, Charlie's Angels, Catwoman* and some of James Bond's women, to name but a few) shows us that a defensive or submissive attitude in the male can well be allied to sexual arousal. The ethologists would call it "appeasement behavior."

This increasing *submission* as arousal rises can be seen to enhance species survival. The higher domination impulse at low levels of arousal allows members of the species to fight off peer competition and even to test the prowess or perseverance of the suitor in the face of opposition. But if this aggressive behavior were to increase proportionately as mating proceeded, the couple would end up making war, not love. If, on the other hand, the submissive impulse builds up faster than the aggressive impulse (as seems to be the case) the resulting interaction is less painful and more fun. Such a concept sheds new light on the popular belief that "good sex often follows a fight," by transforming it into "good sex is often the accompaniment of ceasing to be aggressive." It also explains why a woman (and sometimes a man) might protest at the partner's aggressive advances at the beginning of a passage of arms, only to welcome the same treatment at a later stage of lovemaking.

In the case of the types of variant that we have been studying, however, it would seem that this tendency to submit as arousal mounts has gotten out of hand, for it will be remembered that submissive fantasies were far more popular than dominant ones among all the male variant groups. It seems likely, in fact, that the repression of childhood is manifested in this way—making it impossible for the individual to obtain sexual pleasure except within the context of submission to the authority of the partner. Such a pattern would, perhaps, be less readily identified as abnormal among women.

CHANGING THE SCRIPT

Very often when a variant man wishes to incorporate his partner into a dramatic scenario he finds her either unwilling as actress or as audience. In our experience, a woman can seldom immediately accept variant behavior from a man, even if she herself has the seeds of it. If she can and does, of course, there is no problem; if she cannot, however, then, if the matter is not to be side-stepped altogether (as does sometimes occur, though not always with happy results), the script of one partner or the other may need to be changed.

Examination of the methods by which "author" and "audience" (i.e. the variant male and the generally nonvariant female partner) may be brought together shows a definite change of emphasis over the last twenty years or so. At the beginning of this period, there was an almost automatic assumption that it was the variant's *behavior* that had to be changed, with little regard for the mental processes that accompanied it and an almost total disregard for the nature and flexibility of the partner's attitude. The possibility that the partner might accept or even—with a little persuasion—go along with her man's predilection was never really explored. Thus the man was almost certainly referred for treatment of some kind.

The traditional psychoanalytic technique has largely fallen into disrepute nowadays among academic psychologists, because it is recognized that it is all too easily marred by over-interpretation of the patient's statements. Paradoxically, the modern approach to therapy, that of attempting to modify patients' behavior by rewarding "desirable" behavior and punishing "undesirable" behavior, may be open to a similar criticism, that the choice of treatments used and the changes that are deemed desirable tell us as much about the personality of the therapist as that of the patient. Behavior therapy nevertheless has the advantage that we can measure any

change in that behavior and thus form an objective opinion as
to the effectiveness of the method, rather than having to rely
on the therapist's subjective judgment of that improvement.

A fairly full description of the methods used to eliminate or
reduce variant behavior has been provided by Wilson (1978):
for the sake of completeness, however, a brief description of
the relevant treatments follows.

Aversion therapy derives from an application of the "carrot
and stick" principle, but here the stick is more evident than
the carrot. For example, a transvestite may be told to cross-
dress in his favorite costume; when he proceeds to do so,
however, he receives an unpleasant but nondangerous electric shock, terminating the moment he starts to remove the
female clothing. The process is repeated a number of times,
so that the act of cross-dressing becomes associated with an
unpleasant physical and emotional state and is therefore reduced in frequency.

Systematic desensitization is a scientifically organized version of gradually getting used to something disliked, and is
consequently used more for removing phobias than for treating predilections. Since in a number of cases a variant behavior has persisted because the patient is terrified of
approaching a woman for direct sexual purposes rather than
out of any positive compulsion towards the variation itself,
systematic desensitization can, in such cases, be used to good
effect. Much of the therapy of Masters and Johnson is based
on the very real fact that some sexual dysfunctions such as
impotence, frigidity, premature ejaculation and vaginismus
are due to the couple being frightened of one another or even
of the opposite sex as a whole. It therefore makes explicit use
of systematic desensitization principles. Initially, the couple
are expressly forbidden to have any form of sexual activity.
After this anxiety-reducing period, they are encouraged to receive and give pleasure to each other with expressions of
closeness, warmth, touching and pleasing each other without
indulging in direct genital activity. Later, when an ambience
of intimacy, trust and relaxation has been established, contact

with the genital areas, but not intercourse, is commenced and explored. Intercourse is thus approached very gradually, with no anxiety-producing pressures present, and the reward of orgasm for both partners is thus much more easily and frequently obtained. Like most therapy systems, the Masters and Johnson technique contains many components beyond those which we have described, but much of the therapeutic process is clearly based on the principles of systematic desensitization.

Behavior modification alone may be effective, but both treatment and result may be improved if thoughts, attitudes and fantasies are deliberately manipulated at the same time. There are several methods of manipulation.

Thought-stopping is another scientific application of a commonsense idea, this time that of thinking about something else. The therapist first establishes the nature of other interests possessed by the patient, together with any attendant fantasies concerning those interests which either already exist or can be composed. The undesirable variant fantasy is now summoned up, the therapist calls "Stop!" and the patient switches immediately to the previously agreed-upon alternative attractive fantasy. After doing this a number of times in the clinic, the patient is told to practice at home the sequence of calling up the variant fantasy, then stopping it himself by a deliberate self-command. Such a technique would of course never actually work unless some reward were provided for changing horses in mid-stream, so the technique has been found most useful in cases where the success of intercourse is being marred by the intrusion of the variant fantasy. It doesn't necessarily totally obliterate the fantasy, but merely puts it under control, with the reward of an orgasm every time the process is successfully carried out.

Covert sensitization is a sort of aversion therapy without physical punishment, using a fantasy related to the variation to symbolize the "undesirable" behavior and another unpleasant (consequential) fantasy to serve as the punishment. A masochist, for example, might have his masochistic desires lessened by repeatedly associating his favorite erotic scene with a "follow-up" of his children discovering him in mid-session, or his employer confronting him with a set of compromising photographs of the patient playing out his fantasies. Such methods at least seem a little more humane than those involving physical persuasion, and may backfire less readily than the story often quoted to us—but nonetheless probably apocryphal—of the masochist who was treated by an attractive female therapist by direct aversion therapy and who consequently lost all desire to be beaten by his childhood schoolteacher but became highly attached to the idea of being strapped to a chair and given electric shocks by the therapist!

Fantasy-reshaping has echoes of the anecdote above, but can be used more constructively: to some extent it is a modification of the thought-stopping process described earlier. In this technique, patients are instructed to begin masturbating to their favorite variant fantasy until orgasm is inevitable. At this point, their task is to switch to another fantasy that has been previously agreed upon as more desirable. After doing this successfully four or five times, they are instructed to start moving the onset of the desirable fantasy to a point earlier in the masturbation sequence, thus shifting the variant fantasy backwards in time until it is entirely unnecessary to the arousal of the patients. Thus the patients learn to masturbate without the aid of their variant fantasy. More recently, this technique for reshaping fantasies has been supplemented with the use of visual and audio erotica to strengthen the power of the competing, desirable fantasies and penis volume measurements have been taken to monitor progress. With these additions, Marshall (1973) reports successful treatment of eleven out of twelve male variants (three homosexuals, two exhibitionists, two fetishists, two rapists and three pedophiles).

Whether the patient is bullied or wooed away from one behavior and toward another, all these techniques have in common the idea that sex in at least some forms is permitted. People are placed in a situation where of course it's all right to talk about it, to watch pornographic films, to masturbate. The attitude is not so much that permission is being given (which is quite powerful in itself to people who have been told by many another authority figure that permission most certainly cannot be given) but that it never occurred to anyone in their right mind that permission could ever be withheld. Such a liberated attitude is certainly conducive to change, and that is a good first step, for it is likely to reduce the anxiety of the patient at being what he is, even if he knows that he is visiting the therapist in order to become something else.

THE OTHER SIDE OF THE COIN

"There is no such thing," wrote Masters and Johnson (1970), "as an uninvolved partner in any marriage in which there is some form of sexual inadequacy." Substitute "relationship" for "marriage" and "variancy" for "inadequacy," and you would probably have the view of a very large proportion of our subjects, even though some of them would perhaps be indulging in wishful thinking. However, since female partners do not come to therapists to acquire a variant behavior in the way that some variants come to rid themselves of a variant behavior, we cannot say whether behavior modification works as well on women under those conditions.

Nevertheless, a fair proportion of our subjects' partners know of, tolerate and even in some measure understand their man's sexual position, a number of these accepting women cooperate in playing out his special sexual script and some obtain real sexual pleasure by participating. And since constitutionally primed female variants are so rare, it seems likely that some women can and do learn to like these variations later in life. Yet while we have on many occasions discussed the matter with variants and their partners, we still find ourselves somewhat at a loss in attempting to advise any variant who asks us how he should go about helping a partner to understand, tolerate, cooperate with or actively enjoy his own

particular sexual script. Certain of the difficulties in even beginning communication on the subject are themselves due to
upbringing and are very difficult to change. The man may find
it too anxiety-provoking even to tell his partner of his variant
pattern, and, if he does manage to do so, his partner may find
it too anxiety-provoking to continue the discussion.

Obviously, little interaction can take place under these circumstances. However, we believe that in today's more tolerant climate, a rational discussion of the situation should be
possible. When we embarked upon the work that has formed
the substance of this book, we had no wish either to denigrate
variants or their activities, nor did we seek to advocate variant
behavior. Our results seem to show that our variant is a little
more introverted, a little more anxious and emotional, a little
less equipped with socio-sexual skills than the average man of
his age, and that the woman who partners him either professionally or for love often compensates for this reserve. On the
other hand, it cannot be said that the broad mass of fetishists,
transvestites and sadomasochists that we have studied resemble the classical models of neurotic, psychotic and psychopath
in anything more than imputation. We have noted the frequently submissive nature of the sexual role that many of our
subjects like to play, whether the fantasy partner takes a particularly aggressive role or not. We have learned that most
sadomasochists are probably very much less dangerous than
society believes them to be, and have pondered on whether
the transvestite is merely the victim of an emasculating low
libido. We have observed that dominant and submissive attitudes in people are to some extent independent and argued
the possibility of both males and females becoming more submissive as their libido rises during lovemaking. We have
noted to what extent, and by what possible mechanism sexual
variations are learned and the extent to which they may be
inborn. These ideas and findings lead us to believe that the
variant is nothing more than a person who by virtue of innate
predispositional attitudes and certain types of upbringing has
gravitated toward a type of sexual pattern which seemed in
the comparative innocence of puberty to be quite natural to

him, and that, in short, "to be sexually different is not all that different."

Discussion of sexual variancy between partners should not, therefore, *need* to be accompanied by tension and rejection on one side, nor by defensiveness and resentment, if discussion is rejected, on the other. The point is made simply because we believe from interviews and conversations with variants and their partners that the freedom to discuss feelings, to tease one another, to puzzle over individual differences and to accept the existence of the other's sexual preference without rancor is worth more to the couple than any subsequent "cooperation," without internal motivation, on the nonvariant partner's part. Such a discussion of variant behavior may, if either partner prefers, be initiated on the neutral ground of a counseling center, but perhaps should not be subsequently confined to that situation.

For some, mutual enjoyment of a variant activity will probably never be possible or even desirable. "The switch that turns him on is precisely the one that turns me off," one woman told us without emotion. The conditioning model which rewards variant behavior with increased sexual pleasure, as often happens, may become a two-edged sword in the hand of any man whose partner equates the mode of variant behavior with her man's sexual excitement. With such a final reckoning she may not unjustifiably conclude that her man is in love with the variant activity and not with her. Over and over again, couples who *both* enjoy a variant activity (the woman having learned the behavior from the man and found it rewarding) have stressed the necessity of creating an ambience of love, trust and the desire to please rather than be pleased, in order to allow "variations on the theme of love" to flourish. The occasions on which such a technique was found repeatedly to fail are never cited, yet from private communications we have realized that, for some women, the creation of such an atmosphere is merely regarded by them as "an attempt to soften me up, a trick to con me into something I just don't like doing."

Should persuasion, then, ever take place? We do not know,

for here is an area where the psychologist's generalization should yield to the feelings of the individual couple. Perhaps, though, a little persuasion and a similar degree of cooperation should be undertaken, for it might help to develop a line of communication between lovers which compensates for any weakness induced either by personality predisposition or up-bringing and environment.

Bibliography

Bannister, D., and Fransella, F., *Inquiring Man,* Harmondsworth: Penguin Books, 1971.

Barclay, A. M., "The effect of female aggressiveness on aggressive and sexual fantasies," *Journal of Projective Techniques and Personality Assessment,* 1970 (34), 19–26.

Barclay, A. M., and Haber, R. N., "The relation of aggressive to sexual motivation," *Journal of Personality,* 1965 (33), 462–75.

Benjamin, H., *The Transsexual Phenomenon,* New York: The Julian Press, 1966.

Buhrich, N., and McConaghy, N., "Can fetishism occur in transsexuals?" *Archives of Sexual Behaviour,* 1977 (6), 3, 223–35.

Buhrich, N., and McConaghy, N., "The discrete syndromes of transvestism and transsexualism," *Archives of Sexual Behaviour,* 1977 (6), 6, 483–95.

Byrne, D., and Lamberth, J., "The effect of erotic stimuli on sex arousal, evaluative responses and subsequent behaviour," in *Technical Report of the Commission on Obscenity and Pornography,* Vol. III, Washington, D.C.: U.S. Government Printing Office, 1971.

Epstein, A. W., "Relationship of fetishism and transvestism to brain and particularly to temporal lobe dysfunction," *Journal of Nervous and Mental Disease,* 1961 (133), 247–53.

Eysenck, H. J., *Sex and Personality,* London: Open Books, 1976.

Eysenck, H. J., and Nias, D. K. B., *Sex, Violence and the Media*, New York: Harper Colophon Books, 1979.

Eysenck, H. J., and Wilson, G. D., *The Psychology of Sex*, London: J. M. Dent, 1979.

Freeman, G., *The Undergrowth of Literature*, London: Thomas Nelson and Sons, 1967.

Freud, S., (1927) "Fetishism," in *Standard Edition of Freud's Works*, Vol. XXI, London and New York: Hogarth Press, 1961.

Gagnon, J., *Human Sexualities*, Glenview, Illinois: Scott-Foresman, 1977.

Gorman, G. F., "Fetishism occurring in identical twins," *British Journal of Psychiatry*, 1964 (110), 255–6.

Gosselin, C., "Personality attributes of the average rubber fetishist," in M. Cook and G. D. Wilson (eds.), *Proceedings of the First International Conference on Love and Attraction*, London: Pergamon Press, 1979.

Gosselin, C., and Eysenck, S. B. G., "The transvestite 'double image': a preliminary report," *Personality and Individual Differences*, 1980 (1), 172–73.

Hirschfield, M., *Sexual Anomalies and Perversions*, London: Francis Aldor, 1946.

Holbrook, D., *Sex and Dehumanisation*, London: Pitman Publishing, 1972.

Kinsey, A. C., Pomeroy, W. B., and Martin, C. E., *Sexual Behavior in the Human Male*, Philadelphia and London: W. B. Saunders Co., 1948

Kinsey, A. C., Pomeroy, W. B., Martin, C. E., and Gebhardt, P. H., *Sexual Behavior in the Human Female*, New York: Simon and Schuster, 1965.

Krafft-Ebing, R., (1886) *Psychopathia Sexualis*, translation, New York: Stein and Day, 1965.

Laing, R. D., *The Divided Self*, London: Tavistock Publications, 1960.

Langevin, R., and Martin, M., "Can erotic responses be classically conditioned," *Behaviour Therapy*, 1975 (6), 350–5.

McGuire, R. J., Carlisle, J. M., and Young, B. G., "Sexual deviations as conditioned behaviour: a hypothesis," *Behaviour Research and Therapy*, 1965 (2), 185–90.

Marshall, W. L., "The modification of sexual fantasies: a combined treatment approach to the reduction of deviant sexual behaviour," *Behaviour Research and Therapy*, 1973 (11), 557–64.

Money, J., Hampson, J. G., and Hampson, J. L., "Imprinting and the establishment of gender role," *Archives of Neurological Psychiatry*, 1957 (77), 333–6.

Money, J., and Brennan, J. G., "Sexual dimorphism in the psychology of female transsexuals," *Journal of Nervous and Mental Diseases,* 1968 (147), 487–99.

Morris, D., *The Human Zoo,* New York: Dell publishing, 1970.

North, M., *The Outer Fringe of Sex,* London: Odyssey Press, 1970.

Oakley, G., *Sex Change and Dress Deviation,* London: Morntide, 1970.

Penfield, W., and Rasmussen, T., *The Cerebral Cortex of Man,* New York: The McMillan Co., 1950.

Rachman, S. J., and Hodgson, R. J., "Experimentally induced 'sexual fetishism,' " *Psychological Record,* 1968 (18), 25–27.

Schachter, S., *Emotion, obesity and crime,* New York: Academic Press, 1971.

Schachter, S., and Singer, J. E., "Cognitive, social and physiological determinants of emotional state," *Psychological Review,* 1962 (69), 377–99.

Stoller, R., "The term transvestism," *Archives of General Psychiatry,* 1971 (24), 330–7.

Stoller, R., *Perversion—the erotic form of hatred,* New York: Delta Books, 1976.

Walters, R. H., Cheyne, J. A., and Banks, R. K. (eds.), *Various Essays on Punishment,* Harmondsworth: Penguin Books, 1972.

West, D. J., *The Young Offender,* Harmondsworth: Penguin Books, 1967.

Wilson, G. D., "Personality," in Eysenck, H. J., and Wilson, G. D. (eds.), *A Textbook of Human Psychology,* Lancaster: MTP Press, 1976.

Wilson, G. D., and Nias, D. K. B., *The Mystery of Love,* New York: Quadrangle, 1976 (English title *Love's Mysteries,* London: Open Books, 1976).

Wilson, G. D., *Secrets of Sexual Fantasy,* London: J. M. Dent, 1978.

Definitions of Statistical Terms

BIMODALITY   The property in a statistical sample of having two modes (divided into two extremes)

CORRELATION COEFFICIENT   A statistical measure of the degree of association between two variables, which varies between 0 and 1. Height and weight, for example, are correlated about 0.7—tall people tend to be heavier. A negative sign before a correlation coefficient means that high scores on one trait tend to be associated with low scores on the other

CUTOFF POINT   In a statistical sample, the point beyond which behavior is abnormal (or numbers are significant)

FACTOR ANALYSIS   A statistical technique by which themes that are similarly rated are grouped together

MEAN RATINGS   Average ratings

MODE   In a statistical sample, the value that occurs most frequently

SCATTERGRAM   A graph showing the location of many points in relation to two variables

STANDARD DEVIATION   A measure of the dispersion of a set of numerical values about their arithmetic mean

Index